T0210614

# Data Profiling

# Synthesis Lectures on Data Management

Editor
**H.V. Jagadish,** *University of Michigan*

Founding Editor
**M. Tamer Özsu,** *University of Waterloo*

*Synthesis Lectures on Data Management* is edited by H.V. Jagadish of the University of Michigan. The series publishes 80–150 page publications on topics pertaining to data management. Topics include query languages, database system architectures, transaction management, data warehousing, XML and databases, data stream systems, wide scale data distribution, multimedia data management, data mining, and related subjects.

Data Profiling

Ziawasch Abedjan, Lukasz Golab, Felix Naumann, and Thorsten Papenbrock

ISBN: 978-3-031-00737-8     paperback
ISBN: 978-3-031-01865-7     ebook
ISBN: 978-3-031-00092-8     hardcover

DOI 10.1007/978-3-031-01865-7

A Publication in the Springer series
*SYNTHESIS LECTURES ON DATA MANAGEMENT*

Lecture #52
Series Editor: H.V. Jagadish, *University of Michigan*
Founding Editor: M. Tamer Özsu, *University of Waterloo*
Series ISSN
Print 2153-5418     Electronic 2153-5426

# Data Profiling

Ziawasch Abedjan
Technische Universität Berlin

Lukasz Golab
University of Waterloo

Felix Naumann
Hasso Plattner Institute, University of Potsdam

Thorsten Papenbrock
Hasso Plattner Institute, University of Potsdam

*SYNTHESIS LECTURES ON DATA MANAGEMENT #52*

# ABSTRACT

Data profiling refers to the activity of collecting data about data, i.e., metadata. Most IT professionals and researchers who work with data have engaged in data profiling, at least informally, to understand and explore an unfamiliar dataset or to determine whether a new dataset is appropriate for a particular task at hand. Data profiling results are also important in a variety of other situations, including query optimization, data integration, and data cleaning. Simple metadata are statistics, such as the number of rows and columns, schema and datatype information, the number of distinct values, statistical value distributions, and the number of null or empty values in each column. More complex types of metadata are statements about multiple columns and their correlation, such as candidate keys, functional dependencies, and other types of dependencies.

This book provides a classification of the various types of profilable metadata, discusses popular data profiling tasks, and surveys state-of-the-art profiling algorithms. While most of the book focuses on tasks and algorithms for relational data profiling, we also briefly discuss systems and techniques for profiling non-relational data such as graphs and text. We conclude with a discussion of data profiling challenges and directions for future work in this area.

# KEYWORDS

data analysis, data modeling, dependency discovery, data mining, metadata

# Contents

# Preface

In 2013, we recognized the significant amount of research that had been and was being invested in automatic and efficient discovery of metadata for (mostly relational) databases. After much work in the 1990s, the field of data profiling was experiencing a renaissance at the time, and we decided to first create a roadmap for future research and then write a survey about the existing literature. The first step, the roadmap, resulted in a SIGMOD Record article [Naumann, 2013], which briefly laid out the existing work and emphasized the need for further work in the areas of interactive data profiling, incremental data profiling, profiling non-relational data, and, finally, performing profiling tasks on modern computer and software architectures. The second step resulted in a *VLDB Journal* survey [Abedjan et al., 2015b], which in turn was presented as tutorials at ICDE'16 [Abedjan et al., 2016] and SIGMOD'17 [Abedjan et al., 2017]. That survey served as a foundation for this synthesis lecture, which significantly extends and updates the material covered there.

Data profiling is an activity that most computer scientists and data analysts have engaged in. That said, the term data profiling is not yet well-known and neither are some of the efficient data profiling algorithms that have recently appeared in the literature. Our aim is to establish data profiling as a branch of computer science, explain its utility in various data preparation tasks, survey the computation challenges in data profiling and how they can be solved, and encourage further research in this field.

We assume that readers possess a basic computer science background, including programming (e.g., data types, object-oriented programming), algorithms and data structures (e.g., hash maps), and relational database systems (e.g., relational model, SQL).

This book is written for students, researchers, and practitioners involved in data-driven projects. We hope it will be useful to software developers who build data intensive backend systems, data scientists who analyze various datasets for patterns, data enthusiasts who share and exchange information, database experts who maintain large collections of data, IT professionals who integrate and clean data, and computer science students who want to improve their data science skills. If you are part of one ore more of these groups, this book is for you!

Ziawasch Abedjan, Lukasz Golab, Felix Naumann, and Thorsten Papenbrock
Berlin, Waterloo, Potsdam, October 2018

# Acknowledgments

We thank all supporters of this book who contributed ideas, technical feedback, and literature material. Most of these wonderful people also collaborated in various data profiling research projects that led up to this book.

1. Anja Jentzsch
2. Arvid Heise
3. Axel Stebner
4. Barna Saha
5. Carl Ambroselli
6. Claudia Exeler
7. Divesh Srivastava
8. Fabian Tschirschnitz
9. Fabian Windheuser
10. Falco Dürsch
11. Fei Chiang
12. Flip Korn
13. Hazar Harmouch
14. Howard Karloff
15. Ihab Ilyas
16. Jakob Zwiener
17. Jana Bauckmann
18. Jannik Marten
19. Jan-Peer Rudolph
20. Jaroslaw Szlichta
21. Jens Ehrlich
22. Jorge-Arnulfo Quiané-Ruiz
23. Martin Schönberg
24. Maxi Fischer
25. Maximilian Grundke
26. Mehdi Kargar
27. Moritz Finke
28. Nils Strelow
29. Paolo Papotti
30. Parke Godfrey
31. Patrick Schulze
32. Philipp Langer
33. Philipp Schirmer
34. Sebastian Kruse
35. Tanja Bergmann
36. Tim Draeger
37. Tim Friedrich
38. Tobias Bleifuß
39. Tommy Neubert
40. Vincent Schwarzer

Our thanks go out especially to the reviewers, who gave us valuable and detailed feedback. Many thanks also to our publisher, Morgan & Claypool, who actively assisted and edited this book, and to our institutions, the Hasso Plattner Institute, the Technische Universität Berlin, and the University of Waterloo, who provided the funding and infrastructure that made writing this book possible.

Last but certainly not least, we thank our families for their support. You are wonderful and this book would not have made it without your patience and help!

Ziawasch Abedjan, Lukasz Golab, Felix Naumann, and Thorsten Papenbrock
October 2018

CHAPTER 1

# Discovering Metadata

Data profiling is the set of activities and processes designed to determine the metadata of a given dataset. These metadata, such as statistics about the data or dependencies among columns, can help understand and manage new datasets. In particular, the advent of "Big Data," with the promise of data science and data analytics, and with the realization that business insight may be extracted from data, has brought many datasets into organizations' data lakes and data reservoirs. Data profiling helps understand and prepare data for subsequent cleansing, integration, and analysis.

This book organizes and explains research results in the area of data profiling. We examine methods to collect basic statistics and to discover complex dependencies. We show various use cases and discuss profiling tools. Finally, we present the challenges ahead of us to achieve truly helpful technology for data-oriented applications.

## 1.1    MOTIVATION AND OVERVIEW

Already in 2012, leading researchers have recognized *"If we just have a bunch of data sets in a repository, it is unlikely anyone will ever be able to find, let alone re-use, any of this data. With adequate metadata, there is some hope, but even so, challenges will remain…"* [Agrawal et al., 2012]. In many cases, these "bunches of data sets" are dumps of databases, raw data files, or document folders. Most often they do not include structural information, documentation, structural or semantic constraints, or any other kind of metadata. There are many possible reasons for a lack of metadata: it is lost during transformation or transportation, it might have never existed, it is outdated, it is incomplete, etc. For instance, many scientific datasets are provided in the form of many csv files, which do include column headers but no definitions of datatypes, keys, or foreign keys, let alone functional dependencies or other statistics.

Data profiling attempts to reconstruct or recreate such metadata, and can be seen as one component of the broader activity of *data preparation*, which also includes data extraction, organization, and curation. A recent article found that data preparation activities consume about 79% of a data scientist's time, and 78% of data scientists declare them to be the least enjoyable part of data science [Press, 2016]. According to Johnson, *"Data profiling refers to the activity of creating small but informative summaries of a database"* [Johnson, 2009]. Thus, data profiling directly supports data preparation for many different use cases, which we describe in more detail later.

Data profiling is an important and frequent activity of any IT professional and researcher. It encompasses a vast array of methods to examine datasets and produce metadata. Among the simpler results are statistics, such as the number of null values and distinct values in a column, its data type, or the most frequent patterns of its data values. Metadata that are more difficult to compute involve multiple columns, such as inclusion dependencies or functional dependencies. Also of practical interest are approximate versions of these dependencies, because they are typically more efficient to compute when exact results are not needed. In this book, however, we concentrate on exact methods, which are often the basis of their approximate versions.

Like many data management tasks, data profiling faces three challenges: (i) ingesting the input, (ii) performing the computation, and (iii) managing and interpreting the output. Apart from typical data formatting issues, the first challenge involves specifying the expected outcome, i.e., determining which profiling tasks to execute on which parts of the data. In fact, many tools require a precise specification of what to inspect. Other approaches are more open and perform a wider range of tasks, discovering all metadata automatically.

The second challenge is the focus of this book and that of most research efforts in data profiling. The computational complexity of data profiling algorithms depends on the number of rows and columns. Many tasks need to inspect all column combinations, i.e., their complexity is exponential in the number of columns. In addition, the scalability of data profiling methods is important, as the ever-growing data volumes demand disk-based and distributed processing.

The third challenge is arguably the most difficult, namely meaningfully interpreting data profiling results. In general, we assume the dataset itself as our only input, which means that we cannot rely on query logs, schema, documentation, etc. Thus, any discovered metadata refer only to the given data instance and cannot be used to derive schematic/semantic properties with certainty, such as value domains, primary keys, or foreign key relationships. Profiling results need interpretation, which is usually performed by database and domain experts. Where applicable, we point to the few research activities that have addressed this third challenge and we discuss it further in the context of concrete use cases (Chapter 6).

Due to the complexity of metadata discovery, which we classify in the next chapter, most research and much of this book focus on efficient (and scalable) execution of data profiling tasks. Various tools and algorithms have tackled this challenge in different ways. First, they may rely on the capabilities of the underlying database management system (DBMS), as many profiling tasks can be expressed as SQL queries. Second, innovative techniques have been proposed to handle specific computational challenges, for instance using indexing schemes, parallel processing, and reusing intermediate results. Third, several methods have been proposed that deliver only approximate results for various profiling tasks, for instance by profiling samples. Finally, users may be asked to narrow down the discovery process to certain columns or tables. For instance, some tools verify inclusion dependencies on user-suggested pairs of columns, but cannot automatically check inclusion between all pairs of columns or column sets.

Systematic data profiling outside of academia, i.e., profiling beyond the occasional exploratory SQL query or spreadsheet browsing, is usually performed with dedicated tools or components, such as IBM's Information Analyzer, Microsoft's SQL Server Integration Services (SSIS), or Informatica's Data Explorer. Chapter 8 gives an overview of such tools. Systematic data profiling usually proceeds as follows. First, the user specifies the data to be profiled and selects the types of metadata to be generated. Next, the tool computes the metadata in batch-mode, using SQL queries and/or specialized algorithms. Depending on the volume of the data and the selected profiling results, this step can last minutes to hours. Results are usually displayed in a collection of tabs, tables, charts, and other visualizations to be explored by the user. Finally, the discovered metadata (or the relevant parts of it) are applied to concrete use cases. Data cleaning is one such use case, where the discovered patterns and dependencies may be translated to constraints or rules that are then enforced in a subsequent cleansing/integration phase. For instance, after discovering that the most frequent pattern for phone numbers is (ddd)ddd-dddd, this pattern can be promoted to a *rule* stating that all phone numbers must be formatted accordingly. Most data cleansing tools either transform differently formatted numbers into the most frequent pattern or mark them as incorrect.

Algorithms developed and published in academia, on the other hand, are usually dedicated to a single, complex task, do not rely on an underlying infrastructure, and do not provide visualization or interpretation capabilities. Exceptions are discussed in Chapter 8.

By far, the largest portion of research and commercial development has focused on tabular, relational data. Consequently, we also focus on such data, but we do cover data profiling for other data models in Chapter 7.

## 1.2    DATA PROFILING AND DATA MINING

A clear, well defined, and accepted distinction between data profiling and data mining does not exist. We believe there are at least two differences.

1. Distinction by the object of analysis: instance vs. schema or columns vs. rows.

2. Distinction by the goal of the task: description of existing data vs. new insights beyond existing data.

Following the first criterion, Rahm and Do distinguish data profiling from data mining by the number of columns that are examined: "data profiling focuses on the instance analysis of individual attributes. […] Data mining helps discover specific data patterns in large datasets, e.g., relationships holding between several attributes" [Rahm and Do, 2000]. While this distinction is well defined, we believe that tasks such as discovering functional dependencies are part of data profiling, even if they discover relationships between multiple columns.

We believe a different distinction along both criteria is more useful: data profiling gathers technical metadata from *columns* to support data management; data mining and data analytics discovers non-obvious results from *rows* to support business management with new insights. For instance, typical data profiling results, such as keys, data types, and dependencies, are all expressed in terms of schema elements, namely columns, or describe constraints on columns. On the other hand, typical data mining results, such as clustering or prediction models, are expressed in terms of records or rows, i.e., they explain relationships between multiple rows. However, the distinction is fuzzy: for example, data summarization, which is a sub-area of data mining aiming to discover a concise set of tuples or frequent patterns that accurately represent a dataset, overlaps with data profiling. Given this distinction, we concentrate on data profiling and put aside the broad area of data mining, which has already received unifying treatment in numerous textbooks [Han et al., 2011] and surveys [Ceglar and Roddick, 2006].

Data mining surveys include an overview by Chen et al., who discuss the kinds of databases (relational, OO, temporal, etc.), the kinds of knowledge to be mined (association rules, clustering, deviation analysis, etc.), and the kinds of techniques to be used [Chen et al., 1996]. We follow a similar plan in this book. In particular, we describe the different classes of data profiling tasks and we examine various techniques to perform them.

## 1.3    USE CASES

As part of data preparation, data profiling has many traditional use cases, including basic interpretation of profiling results to support data exploration, making direct use of discovered constraints, for instance in data cleansing or query optimization, and deriving meaning from the results, such as in schema engineering. Below, we briefly explain a few popular use cases. Chapter 6 examines these and others in more detail.

**Data exploration**  When datasets arrive at an organization and/or accumulate in so-called data lakes, experts need a basic understanding of their content. Manual data exploration, or data gazing,[1] can and should be supported with data profiling techniques, as we cannot assume that all users are SQL experts explorers, but rather they may be "data enthusiasts" without a formal computer science training [Hanrahan, 2012].

**Query optimization**  A basic form of data profiling is the analysis of individual columns in a given table. Typically, the generated metadata include various counts, such as the number of values, the number of unique values, and the number of non-null values. These metadata are often part of the basic statistics gathered by a DBMS. An optimizer uses them to estimate the selectivity of operators and perform other optimization steps. Mannino et al. give a survey of statistics collection and its relationship to database optimization [Mannino et al., 1988]. More advanced techniques use histograms of value distributions, functional dependencies, and unique column combinations to optimize range-queries [Poosala et al., 1996] or for dynamic reoptimization [Kache et al., 2006].

---

[1]"Data gazing involves looking at the data and trying to reconstruct a story behind these data. [...] Data gazing mostly uses deduction and common sense" [Maydanchik, 2007].

**Database reverse engineering** Given a "bare" database instance, the task of schema and database reverse engineering is to identify its relations and attributes, as well as domain semantics, such as foreign keys and cardinalities [Markowitz and Makowsky, 1990, Petit et al., 1994]. Hainaut et al. call these metadata "implicit constructs," i.e., those that are not explicitly specified by DDL statements [Hainaut et al., 2009]. However, possible sources for reverse engineering are DDL statements, data instances, data dictionaries, etc. The result of reverse engineering might be an entity-relationship model or a logical schema to assist experts in maintaining, integrating, and querying the database.

**Data integration** Often, datasets that need to be integrated are unfamiliar and the integration expert wants to explore the datasets first: How large are they, what data types are needed, what are the semantics of columns and tables, are there dependencies between tables and among databases, etc.? The vast abundance of (linked) *open data* and the desire and potential to integrate them with local data has amplified this need.

Apart from exploring individual sources, data profiling can also reveal how and how well two datasets can be integrated. For instance, inclusion dependencies across tables from different sources suggest which tables might reasonably be combined with a join-operation. Additionally, specialized data profiling techniques can reveal how much two relations overlap in their intent and extent.

**Data quality/data cleansing** A frequent and commercially relevant use case is profiling data to prepare a *data cleansing* process. Commercial data profiling tools are usually bundled with corresponding data quality/data cleansing software. Profiling as a data quality assessment tool reveals data errors, such as inconsistent formatting within a column, missing values, or outliers. Profiling results can also be used to measure and monitor the quality of a dataset, for instance by determining the number of records that do not conform to previously established constraints [Kandel et al., 2012, Pipino et al., 2002]. Constraints and dependencies also allow for rule-based data imputation.

**Big data analytics** "Big data," with its high volume, high velocity, and high variety [Laney, 2001], is data that cannot be managed with traditional techniques, which underscores the importance of data profiling. Fetching, storing, querying, and integrating big data is expensive, despite many modern technologies. Before exposing an infrastructure to Twitter's firehose, it might be worthwhile to know about properties of the data one is receiving; before downloading significant parts of the linked data cloud, some prior sense of the integration effort is needed; before augmenting a warehouse with text mining results, an understanding of its data quality is required.

In summary, knowledge about data types, keys, foreign keys, and other constraints supports data modeling and helps keep data consistent, improves query optimization, and reaps all the other benefits of structured data management. Others have mentioned query formulation and indexing [Sismanis et al., 2006] and scientific discovery [Huhtala et al., 1999] as further motivation for data profiling. Also, compression techniques internally perform basic data profiling to optimize the compression ratio. Finally, data governance and data life-cycle management are becoming relevant to businesses trying to adhere to regulations and code. Especially concerned are financial institutions and health care organizations. Again, data profiling can help ascertain which actions to take on which data. Chapter 6 of this book discusses some of these use cases and application areas in more detail.

## 1.4    ORGANIZATION OF THIS BOOK

The goal of this book is to convey a basic understanding of data profiling technologies, in particular the data structures and algorithms. The first half of the book (Chapters 2–6) is dedicated to traditional data profiling tasks, while the second half (Chapters 5–10) introduces more recent and more advanced work.

Chapter 2 provides a taxonomy of data profiling tasks and serves as a guide to the main chapters of this book. Chapter 3 discusses single-column profiling, e.g., statistical measures, such as column distinctness and value distributions. Chapter 4 is the most extensive chapter of the book, covering discovery algorithms for the three most important types of dependencies in the literature: unique column combinations, functional dependencies, and inclusion dependencies. For each, we examine the search space, useful data structures and several algorithmic alternatives.

Chapter 5 revisits the dependencies of the previous chapter and discusses how to relax their strict semantics and make their discovery more useful in practice, where data are not always clean. In addition, we explore other, more advanced types of dependencies, such as order dependencies and denial constraints. Again, algorithmic insights accompany each type of dependency. In Chapter 6 we discuss concrete use cases for data profiling results. In Chapter 7 we leave the relational model behind and explore how the concept of data profiling extends to other data models, such as XML, RDF, and textual data. Chapter 8 then introduces a selection of commercial and academic tools dedicated to data profiling. Chapter 9 discusses open challenges in data profiling, including non-functional challenges such as scalability and efficiency, and functional challenges such as profiling dynamic data. We conclude the book with Chapter 10.

CHAPTER 2

# Data Profiling Tasks

Data profiling is clearly not a single task or problem, but comprises a large and diverse set of tasks. They can be classified by the kind of data they address. Figure 2.1 shows our taxonomy, which, just like this entire book, emphasizes relational data. It classifies tasks into those which consider individual columns, those which identify dependencies across columns, and those which examine non-relational data such as trees, graphs or text. The classes are explained in the following subsections, where we also discuss the relationship between data profiling and data mining.

## 2.1    SINGLE-COLUMN ANALYSIS

A basic form of data profiling is the analysis of individual columns in a given table. Typically, the generated metadata comprises various counts, such as the number of values (size), the number of distinct values (cardinality, distinctness), the number of non-null values (completeness), and the maximum and minimum values. In addition, basic single-column profiling includes histograms and value distributions. Single-column metadata are gathered by DBMSs for query optimization, and provide data scientists with basic understanding of the data at hand, allowing them to effectively read, write, and maintain the data.

More complex analysis, beyond simple counts, reveals more high-level metadata, such as the syntactic data type, possibly restricted to distinguishing strings vs. numeric and dates, and typical patterns in the data values in the form of regular expressions [Raman and Hellerstein, 2001]. Typical data profiling tools display such results and can suggest actions, such as declaring a column with only unique values to be a candidate key or using the most frequent patterns for data cleaning.

In addition to purely syntactic metadata, data profiling can also be used to predict the semantic data type or domain of a given column, i.e., distinguish first_name from product_name from phone_number, etc. Finally, a frequent task of profiling is to create a shorter representation of a column, while retaining as many of its original properties as possible. Such summaries and sketches have been the focus of much research [Cormode et al., 2011], but are not the focus of this book, which mostly addresses exact profiling techniques. Chapter 3 provides more details about these and further single-column profiling tasks.

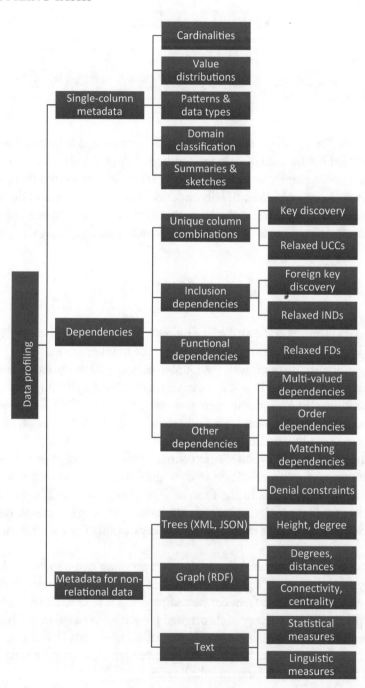

Figure 2.1: **A taxonomy of data profiling tasks.**

## 2.2   DEPENDENCY DISCOVERY

Dependencies are metadata that describe relationships among columns. Typical examples are functional dependencies and inclusion dependencies. The difficulties of automatically discovering such dependencies in a given dataset are threefold. First, the search space of dependency candidates is large, as pairs or even larger combinations of columns must be examined. Second, in principle each candidate requires validation across the entire dataset. Third, the existence of a dependency in the data at hand does not imply that this dependency is meaningful. While most research has addressed the first and second challenge (and is the focus of this book), there is far less work on the semantic interpretation of profiling results.

A typical goal of data profiling is to identify suitable keys for a given table. Thus, the discovery of *unique column combinations* (UCC), i.e., sets of columns whose values uniquely identify rows, is an important data profiling task [Heise et al., 2013]. Once unique column combinations have been discovered, a second step is to identify the intended primary key of a relation.

A frequent real-world use case of multi-column profiling is the discovery of foreign keys [Lopes et al., 2002, Rostin et al., 2009] with the help of *inclusion dependencies* (IND) [Bauckmann et al., 2007, Marchi et al., 2002]. An inclusion dependency states that all values or value combinations from one set of columns also appear in the other set of columns—a prerequisite for a foreign key.

Another form of dependency, which is, inter alia, relevant for data quality work, are *functional dependencies* (FD). A functional dependency states that values in one set of columns functionally determine the value of another column for all rows. Again, much research has been performed to automatically detect FDs [Huhtala et al., 1999, Papenbrock et al., 2015b, Yao and Hamilton, 2008]. Chapter 4 surveys dependency discovery algorithms in detail.

Dependencies have many applications. An obvious use case for functional dependencies is schema normalization. Inclusion dependencies can suggest how to join two relations, possibly across data sources. Their conditional counterparts help explore the data by focusing on certain parts of the dataset. And any dependency can be turned into a rule to check for errors in the data and to improve data quality. We present a variety of algorithms for the discovery of the three most prominent types of dependencies, namely unique column combinations, functional dependencies, and inclusion dependencies, in Chapter 4. Then, after a discussion of relaxed dependencies and more complex dependencies in Chapter 5, we survey further use cases for dependencies in Chapter 6.

## 2.3   RELAXED DEPENDENCIES

Real datasets usually contain exceptions to rules. To account for this, dependencies and other constraints detected by data profiling can be relaxed. Relaxation can take place in two dimensions: relaxing the set of rows that the dependency shall be valid for (e.g., partial and conditional dependencies) or relaxing the equality constraints to compare values (e.g., matching or order dependencies) [Caruccio et al., 2016].

*Partial dependencies* hold for only a subset of the records, for instance, for 95% of the records or for all but 10 records. Such dependencies are valuable in data cleansing scenarios as they describe patterns that hold for almost all records, and thus should probably hold for *all* records if the data were clean. Violating records can be extracted and cleansed [Stonebraker et al., 2013].

The term *approximate* dependency is often used synonymously with *partial* dependency in literature although, strictly speaking, this term has a different meaning. Both partial and approximate dependencies relax the extent, i.e., the scope of a dependency w.r.t. a subset of rows. However, partial dependencies describe their scope either as number, collection, or percentage of records that they are valid for; approximate dependencies are the result of approximate discovery algorithms and can, therefore, at best give only an upper bound for their error. Techniques used in approximate discovery algorithms are, inter alia, sampling [Ilyas et al., 2004] or other summarization techniques [Cormode et al., 2011]. Thus, approximate dependencies are usually much easier to discover than exact dependencies, while partial dependencies are harder to discover than their exact counterparts. Approximate statements are, however, often sufficient for certain tasks, such as data linkage or data exploration, and they can also be used as input to more rigorous discovery tasks of detecting true dependencies. Since approximate discovery is usually easier than exact discovery (e.g., simply run the exact algorithm on a subset of the input), this book does not discuss such approximation techniques in detail.

Once a partial dependency has been detected, it is interesting to characterize for which records it holds, i.e., if we can find a condition that selects precisely those records for which the dependency is valid. *Conditional dependencies* specify such conditions. For instance, a conditional unique column combination might state that the column street is unique for all records with city = `NY'. Conditional inclusion dependencies (CINDs) were proposed by Bravo et al. for data cleaning and contextual schema matching [Bravo et al., 2007]. Conditional functional dependencies (CFDs) were introduced in Fan et al. [2008b], also for data cleaning.

Some dependencies relax the equality constraint for value comparisons. A traditional (exact) functional dependency, for example, demands that if any two records have same values for the attributes of the FD's left-hand side, they also need to have same values for the attribute of the FD's right-hand side. In contrast, a relaxed FD might replace equalities with, for instance, a similarity requirement (*matching dependency*), an ontology look-up (*ontology dependency*), or an inequality condition (*order dependency*). Dependency relaxation and discovery algorithms for such relaxed dependencies are the focus of Chapter 5.

CHAPTER 3

# Single-Column Analysis

In this chapter, we examine the simplest profiling tasks, which are those that analyze individual columns independently. Table 3.1 lists some common single-column profiling tasks that we describe in more detail in the first part of this chapter. The second part discusses technical details and usage scenarios for certain single column profiling tasks. We refer the interested reader to Maydanchik [2007], a book addressing practitioners, for further information about single-column profiling.

## 3.1 CARDINALITIES

Cardinalities refer to numbers that summarize simple metadata. The most basic piece of metadata is the number of rows in a table (num-rows). This corresponds to the number of entities, such as customers, orders, or products, which are present in the table, and is collected by virtually all database management systems to estimate query costs or to assign storage space.

Data profiling tools pay special attention to the number of empty or null values (null-values) within a column to characterize data (in)completeness and therefore data quality.[1] Moreover, the number of distinct values (distinct) is of interest. For data analysts, this number indicates how many different values or entities exist, e.g., how many distinct customers have ordered a product or how many distinct products have been purchased. For query optimizers, the number of distinct values is used to estimate join selectivity. Dividing the number of distinct values by the total number of rows gives uniqueness; a column with a uniqueness of one may be a candidate key.

From a computational standpoint, the above statistics can be computed exactly in a single pass over a column and using a small amount of space, with the exception of counting distinct values, which can be done using sorting or hashing.

## 3.2 VALUE DISTRIBUTIONS

The next set of profiling tasks are those that summarize the distribution of values within a column. A common representation, which is used in DBMSs and data profiling and exploration tools, is a histogram. Equi-width histograms divide the possible values into buckets that have the same size (i.e., each bucket represents a value range of the same length, such as one to ten, ten

---

[1] However, subtle issues such as default values complicate the process of quantifying data completeness. We will return to this problem in Section 3.4.

Table 3.1: Overview of single-column profiling

| Category | Task | Task Description |
|---|---|---|
| Cardinalities | num-rows | Number of rows |
| | null values | Number or percentage of null values |
| | distinct | Number of distinct values |
| | uniqueness | Number of distinct values divided by number of rows |
| Value Distributions | histogram | Frequency histograms (equi-width, equi-depth, etc.) |
| | extremes | Minimum and maximum values in a numeric column |
| | constancy | Frequency of most frequent value divided by number of rows |
| | quartiles | Three points that divide (numeric) values into four equal groups |
| | first digit | Distribution of first digit in numeric values; to check Benford's law |
| Data Types, Patterns, and Domains | basic type | Numeric, alphanumeric, date, time, etc. |
| | data type | DBMS-specific data type (varchar, timestamp, etc.) |
| | lengths | Minimum, maximum, median, and average lengths of values within a column |
| | size | Maximum number of digits in numeric values |
| | decimals | Maximum number of decimals in numeric values |
| | patterns | Histogram of value patterns (Aa9...) |
| | data class | Generic semantic data type, such as code, indicator, text, date/time, quantity, identier |
| | domain | Semantic domain, such as credit card, first name, city, phenotype |

to 20, 20–30, etc.). Equi-depth or equi-height histograms define different ranges for different buckets such that the frequencies of values within each bucket are equal. A special case of an equi-depth histogram is one that contains four buckets divided along the four quartiles. Advanced histograms include biased histograms that use different granularities for different fragments of the value range to provide better accuracy (see, e.g., Cormode et al. [2006]).

DBMSs use histograms for query optimization. For example, a histogram can provide a more accurate estimate of query or operator selectivity than a naive method of assuming a uniform distribution throughout the range of values appearing in a column [Ioannidis, 2003]. Additionally, histograms are directly interpretable by users as they summarize the distribution mass and shape. Moreover, some data profiling systems utilize histograms to fit distributions to the data. It may be useful to an analyst to check if the values of some column are (approximately) normally distributed, and, if so, the number of outliers may be returned by, for example, counting the number of datapoints lying more than three standard deviations away from the mean.

The extremes of a numeric column include its maximum and minimum values. These values support the identification of outliers, i.e., datapoints that lie outside an expected range of values.

The constancy of a column is defined as the frequency of the most frequent value divided by the total number of values. An unexpectedly high constancy may indicate that the most frequent value is a pre-defined default value.

Another statistically interesting value distribution is the distribution over the first digits of a set of numeric values. According to Benford's law, the distribution of the first digit $d$ in naturally occurring numeric datasets approximately follows $P(d) = \log_{10}(1 + \frac{1}{d})$ [Benford, 1938]. As a result, the digit "1" is expected to be the most frequent leading digit, followed by "2" and so on. This property has been observed by Benford and others in a variety of numeric datasets, including weights of molecules, sizes of buildings, surface areas of rivers, and electricity bills. In fact, Benford's law has been used to detect accounting fraud and other suspicious features and anomalies in numeric datasets.

Computing frequency distributions and related metrics requires a single pass over a column, with the exception of equi-depth histograms (i.e., those with equal bucket sizes) and quartiles, where sorting can be used to divide the value range into pieces with the same frequency. Similarly, constancy, which requires the count of the most frequent value, can be computed by sorting or hashing the vales in a column.

We end this section by remarking that there are many more statistical properties of values within a column that may be profiled by database systems or data profiling tools. Examples include a frequency distribution of Soundex codes and word or character n-grams, an inverse frequency distribution (i.e., a distribution of the frequency distribution), or the entropy of the distribution [Kang and Naughton, 2003].

## 3.3   DATA TYPES, PATTERNS, AND DOMAINS

In this section, we discuss single-column profiling tasks that focus on data types and patterns. We start with simple tasks, such as determining the basic data types, and proceed to more complex ones, such as determining the semantic domain of a column.

A basic type can be one of: numeric, alphabetic, alphanumeric, date, or time. The fist three can be verified by the presence or absence of numeric or non-numeric characters. Dates and times can be discovered by checking for numbers within certain ranges and for groups of numbers separated by special characters, e.g., time consists of two digits, followed by a colon, followed by two more digits, etc. Of course, date and time can be represented in many formats (12 vs. 24 hour format, including seconds, including milliseconds, etc.), and all of these should be checked when profiling an unfamiliar dataset.

Data management systems allow more specific data types, such as boolean or integer. These can also be easily detected by checking for the presence of numbers, non-numbers, decimals, etc. Furthermore, it is important to select the most specific data type. For example, Boolean columns should be labeled boolean rather than integer, and one should avoid the catch-alls char or varchar whenever possible.

For the data types decimal, float, and double, one can additionally extract the maximum number of digits and decimals to determine size and decimals, respectively. For alphanumeric columns, one should compute various lengths: the maximum, minimum, mean, and median number of characters. These are useful for schema reverse-engineering (e.g., to determine tight data type bounds), outlier detection (e.g., to find single-character person or product names), and format checking (e.g., to ensure that all the values in a date column have the same length, i.e., the same minimum, maximum, and average number of characters).

Having labeled a column with its data type (and associated metadata about length or size), the next step is to identify any frequently occurring patterns of values. For example, if "d" denotes a single digit, then telephone numbers may follow the pattern +dd (ddd) ddd dddd or the regular expression \(\d3\)\-\d3\-\d4).[2] We note that real datasets often contain errors and outliers. Thus, frequent patterns satisfied by most, but not necessarily all, values within a column should be reported. Datapoints that do not conform to a discovered pattern may indicate data quality problems (e.g., ill-formed telephone numbers).

In the context of data profiling, one challenge in frequent pattern mining is to find the right level of generality or granularity. For example, the regular expression .* matches any string and would correctly apply to any alphanumeric column, but it is not informative. On the other hand, the literal expression data matches only the string "data." Several solutions to this problem have appeared in data profiling tools. For example, in Potter's Wheel, Raman et al. suggest fitting a regular expression with the minimal description length (MDL), which they model as a combination of precision, recall and conciseness [Raman and Hellerstein, 2001]. The RelIE

---

[2]A more detailed regular expression, which takes into account the different formatting options and restrictions (e.g., phone numbers cannot begin with a 1), can easily reach 200 characters in length.

system, which was designed for information extraction from text, creates regular expressions based on training data with positive and negative examples [Li et al., 2008]. Fernau provides a characterization of the problem of learning regular expressions from data and presents a learning algorithm for the task [Fernau, 2009]; this work is also a good starting point for further reading. Finally, a recent article by Ilyas et al. shows how to extract syntactic patterns that are simpler than regular expressions but can be discovered much more efficiently [Ilyas et al., 2018].

Identifying the semantic domain of a column is more difficult than finding its data type or its frequent patterns. This is mainly because semantic domains involve the meaning or interpretation of the data rather than its syntactic properties. In general, this task cannot be fully automated, but solutions exist for common domains describing, e.g., persons and locations. For instance, the presence of certain regular expressions may suggest a semantic domain telephone numbers. However, the same regular expressions may also correspond to fax numbers and further analysis may be required to determine which of these two domains applies to a given column. In the research literature, Zhang et al. take a first step toward semantic domain labeling by clustering columns that have the same meaning across the tables of a database [Zhang et al., 2011], which they extend to the particularly difficult area of numeric values in Zhang and Chakrabarti [2013]. In Vogel and Naumann [2011] the authors take the additional step of matching columns to pre-defined semantics from the person domain. We note that identifying semantic domains is not only of general data profiling interest, but also of particular interest to schema matching, i.e., the task of finding semantic correspondences between elements of different database schemata.

## 3.4    DATA COMPLETENESS

In Section 3.1, we pointed out that counting the fraction of null values in a column indicates the extent of data incompleteness. However, there are non-null values, such as default values, which should not be counted toward completeness. In the simplest case, where we know which value is the default value, we can characterize data incompleteness in terms of the sum of null and default values. However, in most practical data profiling situations, the dataset to be profiled is undocumented and unfamiliar to the user or data analyst. Thus, we may not know which values are default values. For example, web forms often include fields whose values must be chosen from pull-down lists. The first value from the pull-down list may be pre-populated on the form, and some users may not replace it with a proper or correct value due to lack of time or privacy concerns. Specific examples include entering 99999 as the zip code of a United States address or leaving "Alabama" as the pre-populated state (in the U.S., Alabama is alphabetically the first state). Of course, for some records, Alabama may be the true state. Again, the point is that a data analyst may not know that 99999 or "Alabama" were the default values provided by the web form.

Detecting such *disguised* default values is difficult. One heuristic solution is to examine one column at a time, and, for each possible value, compute the distribution of the other attribute values [Hua and Pei, 2007]. For example, if Alabama is indeed a disguised default value, we expect a large subset of tuples with state=Alabama (i.e., those whose true state is different) to form an unbiased sample of the whole dataset. A recent system called FAHES uses a similar approach to discover implicit default values and also discovers default values that are outliers [Qahtan et al., 2018]. For example, a negative value such as −1 could be a default value in a column whose other values are all positive; similarly, 99999 could be the default value in a column whose other values are all much smaller (e.g., age or blood pressure).

Another example in which profiling missing data is not trivial involves timestamp columns, which frequently occur in measurement and transaction datasets. In some cases, tuples are expected to arrive regularly, e.g., in datacenter monitoring, every machine may be configured to report its CPU utilization every minute. However, measurements may be lost en route to the database, and overloaded or malfunctioning machines may not report any measurements [Golab et al., 2011b]. In contrast to detecting missing attribute values, here we are interested in estimating the number of missing tuples through timestamp analysis. Thus, the profiling task may be to single out the columns identified as being of type timestamp, and, for those that appear to be distributed uniformly across a range, infer the expected frequency of the underlying data source and estimate the number of missing tuples. Of course, some timestamp columns correspond to application timestamps with no expectation of regularity, rather than data arrival timestamps. For instance, in an online retailer database, order dates and delivery dates may not be scattered uniformly over time.

## 3.5    APPROXIMATE STATISTICS

Some of the tasks described in this chapter can be computed exactly in a single pass over a column using $\mathcal{O}(1)$ space. Others, such as finding the number of distinct values, may require a sort or more memory for maintaining hash tables or other summary data structures. However, some applications of data profiling may tolerate approximate statistics, among them query optimization (which uses distinct counts and other statistics to estimate query execution costs) and profiling highly dynamic data (where statistics quickly become outdated anyway). In this section, we provide a brief discussion of data summaries and sketches for extracting approximate metadata.

The simplest summary is a uniform sample. Sampling can be used to build approximate distributions and histograms, approximately count the number of distinct values, and detect data types and frequently occurring patterns (recall that frequent patterns need not be satisfied by *all* values in a column); see, e.g., Haas et al. [1995]. Of course, some statistics such as minimum and maximum values cannot be reliably computed from a uniform sample and may require more complex approaches.

A sketch is a small summary of a dataset or a column that can provide approximate statistics [Chandola and Kumar, 2007]. Sketches typically use a combination of counters (uniform or non-uniform), samples, and hashings to transform data values to a smaller domain. They have been applied to approximate query answering, data stream processing, and estimating join sizes [Dasu et al., 2006, Garofalakis et al., 2013, Ntarmos et al., 2009]. For example, suppose we have a very large dataset and we want to identify frequently occurring values. One of the earliest such algorithms uses a counter-based approach [Misra and Gries, 1982]. It maintains $k$ counters, each labeled with the value it represents, and returns values that appear at least $\frac{n}{k}$ times, where $n$ is the total number of records. Initially, all counters are set to zero and their labels are blank. The algorithm reads one record at a time. Let $v$ be the value of the current record. If there already exists a counter for $v$, that counter is incremented. Otherwise, if there is at least one counter with a count of zero, this counter now becomes allocated to $v$ and is incremented. Otherwise, if all $k$ counters are non-zero, then *all $k$* counters are decremented. A similar algorithm called *Space Saving* was proposed subsequently. This algorithm handles the case when all $k$ counters are non-zero differently: Space Saving selects the counter with the smallest count, gives it to $v$ and increments it [Metwally et al., 2005]. More recent methods such as the Count-Min Sketch [Cormode and Muthukrishnan, 2005] use a set of independent hash functions to map values onto a smaller space. We refer the interested reader to Cormode et al. [2011] for a more detailed overview of data summaries and sketches.

Of particular interest to data profiling, there is a variety of approximate algorithms for distinct value counting (i.e., cardinality estimation) using sub-linear space and time (see, e.g., Astrahan et al. [1987], Durand and Flajolet [2003], Flajolet and Martin [1985], Flajolet et al. [2007], Whang et al. [1990]). For example, one of the earliest such algorithms, referred to as Flajolet–Martin [Flajolet and Martin, 1985], only requires $\log(d)$ space where $d$ is the number of distinct values appearing in the data. The idea is to use a random hash function that maps values to bit vectors of length $\log(d)$. On average, we expect half the items to hash to bit vectors that end with a zero and the other half to hash to bit vectors that end with a one. Similarly, on average, a quarter of the items should hash to bit vectors that end with two zeros, and so on. In general, $\frac{1}{2^k}$ items should has to bit vectors that end with $k$ zeros. To exploit this observation, the Flajolet-Martin algorithm hashes each item and records the number of zeros the hash ends with. Let $\ell$ be largest number of such trailing zeros. It turns out that a reliable estimate for the number of distinct items is $\frac{2^\ell}{0.77351}$. To improve accuracy, multiple hash functions can be used and the resulting estimates can be averaged. For more details, we refer the reader to a recent paper that experimentally compares various cardinality estimation algorithms [Harmouch and Naumann, 2017].

## 3.6   SUMMARY AND DISCUSSION

In this section, we have described the simplest data profiling tasks, i.e., those which identify useful syntactic and possibly also semantic metadata about individual columns; all these tasks can be computed independently for each column. Single-column profiling tasks are simple, but can be computed efficiently and may provide sufficient information in many profiling usage scenarios.

Most of the approaches mentioned in this chapter can be generalized to projections of multiple columns, e.g., it is straightforward to compute the number of distinct value pairs within two columns. We also note that the per-column metadata discussed in this chapter can be used as a simple first-cut approach to finding similar columns, which, in turn, can reveal possible join paths, join directions and join result sizes. In Chapter 4, we will provide an in-depth discussion of column-level data dependencies, which can find these types of complex relationships but are significantly more computationally expensive than per-column techniques.

CHAPTER 4

# Dependency Discovery

Three popular multi-column dependencies are *unique column combinations* (UCCs), *functional dependencies* (FDs), and *inclusion dependencies* (INDs). They describe different kinds of *key dependencies*, i.e., keys *of* a table, *within* a table, and *between* tables, respectively [Toman and Weddell, 2008]. If the UCCs, FDs, and INDs are known, data scientists and IT professionals can use them to define valid key and foreign-key constraints (e.g., for schema normalization or schema discovery). Traditionally, constraints, such as keys, foreign keys, and functional dependencies, were considered to be intended constraints of a schema and were known at design time. However, many datasets do not come with key dependencies explicitly, which motivates dependency discovery algorithms. Note that in contrast to dependencies that were defined at design time, each discovered dependency only holds for the given relational instance at hand.

To understand how dependency discovery algorithms work, we first define unique column combinations, functional dependencies, and inclusion dependencies. We then discuss the dependency search problem and explain important concepts and data structures, such as search space pruning and position list indexes. We finally survey popular discovery algorithms for UCCs, FDs, and INDs. The intent of the survey is to convey the main idea of each algorithm and to illustrate various fundamental search approaches. The most relevant techniques and concepts—in particular those that are used across different discovery algorithms and also for different types of dependencies, i.e., dependencies other than UCCs, FDs, and INDs—are described in detail. For in-depth explanations and pseudo-code examples of the algorithms, we refer the reader to the corresponding publications. Table 4.1 gives a summary of the discussed algorithms. We focus on *exact* dependency discovery in this chapter and discuss algorithms for the discovery of *relaxed* dependencies in Chapter 5.

## 4.1 DEPENDENCY DEFINITIONS

Since unique column combinations express a restricted form of functional dependencies, we first explain the latter and then discuss the former. Finally, we define inclusion dependencies and their properties.

We use the following notation. $R$ denotes a relational schema, with $r$ denoting an instance of $R$. A schema defines a set of attributes and an instance defines a set of records. For simplicity, we assume the attributes and the records to be ordered (e.g., by their physical order on disk). This allows us to refer to both via index, i.e., $X_i$ denotes the $i$th attribute in $X \subseteq R$ and $t_i$ denotes

Table 4.1: Discovery algorithms for key dependencies

| Dependency | Algorithms | |
|---|---|---|
| UCC Discovery | GORDIAN | [Sismanis et al., 2006] |
| | HCA | [Abedjan and Naumann, 2011] |
| | DUCC | [Heise et al., 2013] |
| | SWAN | [Abedjan et al., 2014b] |
| | HYUCC | [Papenbrock and Naumann, 2017a] |
| FD Discovery | TANE | [Huhtala et al., 1999] |
| | FDEP | [Flach and Savnik, 1999] |
| | DEP-MINER | [Lopes et al., 2000] |
| | FUN | [Novelli and Cicchetti, 2001] |
| | FASTFDS | [Wyss et al., 2001] |
| | FD_MINE | [Yao et al., 2002] |
| | DFD | [Abedjan et al., 2014c] |
| | HYFD | [Papenbrock and Naumann, 2016] |
| IND Discovery | B&B | [Bell and Brockhausen, 1995] |
| | FIND2 | [Koeller and Rundensteiner, 2003] |
| | ZIGZAG | [Marchi and Petit, 2003] |
| | SPIDER | [Bauckmann et al., 2006] |
| | DEMARCHI | [Marchi et al., 2009] |
| | MIND | [Marchi et al., 2009] |
| | CLIM | [Marchi, 2011] |
| | BINDER | [Papenbrock et al., 2015d] |
| | S-INDD | [Shaabani and Meinel, 2015] |
| | MIND2 | [Shaabani and Meinel, 2016] |

the $i$th record in $r$. The ordering also allows us to use the terms *attribute* and *column*, as well as the terms *record*, *tuple*, and *row*, interchangeably.

The number of attributes in $R$ is $|R|$ and the number of records in $r$ is $|r|$. Sets of attributes are denoted by upper-case letters from the end of the alphabet, i.e., $X, Y, Z$ (with $|X|$ denoting the number of attributes in $X$) and individual attributes by upper-case letters from the beginning of the alphabet, i.e., $A, B, C$. For attribute sets $X \subseteq R$, we assume the same ordering as for their schema $R$ so that $X_i$ refers to the $i$-th attribute in $X$. Furthermore, we define $R[X]$ and $t[X]$ as the projection of schema $R$ and record $t$, respectively, on the attribute set $X$. Accordingly, $t_i[A]$

indicates the value of the attribute $A$ of record $t_i$; we call such attribute values of a record its *cells*. We often write $XY$ or $X, Y$ to denote $X \cup Y$, the union of attribute sets $X$ and $Y$.

### 4.1.1   FUNCTIONAL DEPENDENCIES

A *functional dependency* (FD), written as $X \to A$, asserts that all pairs of records with same values in attribute combination $X$ must also have same values in attribute $A$ [Codd, 1971]. Thus, the values in $A$ *functionally depend* on the values in $X$. More formally, functional dependencies are defined as follows [Ullman, 1990].

**Definition 4.1   Functional dependency.**   Given a relational instance $r$ of schema $R$, the *functional dependency* $X \to A$ with $X \subseteq R$ and $A \in R$ is *valid* in $r$ iff $\forall t_i, t_j \in r : t_i[X] = t_j[X] \Rightarrow t_i[A] = t_j[A]$.

We call the determinant part $X$ of an FD the *left-hand side*, in short LHS, and the dependent part $A$ the *right-hand side*, in short RHS. Moreover, an FD $X \to A$ is a *generalization* of another FD $Y \to A$ if $X \subset Y$ and it is a *specialization* if $X \supset Y$. Functional dependencies with the same LHS, such as $X \to A$ and $X \to B$, can be grouped so that we write $X \to A, B$ or $X \to Y$ for attributes $A$ and $B$ with $\{A, B\} = Y$. Using this notation, Armstrong formulated the following three axioms for functional dependencies on attribute sets $X$, $Y$, and $Z$ [Armstrong, 1974, Beeri and Bernstein, 1979].

1. *Reflexivity*: If $Y \subseteq X$ then $X \to Y$.

2. *Augmentation*: If $X \to Y$ then $X \cup Z \to Y \cup Z$.

3. *Transitivity*: If $X \to Y$ and $Y \to Z$ then $X \to Z$.

An FD $X \to Y$ is *trivial* if $Y \subseteq X$ because all such FDs are valid according to Armstrong's reflexivity axiom; vice versa, the FD is *non-trivial* if $X \nsubseteq Y$ and *fully non-trivial* if $X \cap Y = \emptyset$. Furthermore, an FD is *minimal* if no attribute $B$ exists such that $X \setminus B \to A$ is a valid FD, i.e., if no valid generalization exists. Given all minimal FDs of some relational instance $r$, we can logically infer all other FDs of $r$ with Armstrong's augmentation rule: all LHS-subsets are non-dependencies and all LHS-supersets are true, non-minimal dependencies. We can furthermore generate all trivial FDs with Armstrong's reflexivity rule. Hence, it suffices to discover all minimal, non-trivial FDs with a profiling algorithm; this set covers all true FDs of $r$.

Since keys uniquely determine all other attributes, they are the most popular kind of FDs, i.e., a key $X$ implies a functional dependency $X \to R \setminus X$. Functional dependencies also arise naturally from causal real-world dependencies described in relational datasets. For instance, a product in a catalog functionally defines its manufacturer, the travel time of a specific trip defines the average travel speed, and a package's weight and size jointly define shipping costs.

## 4.1.2   UNIQUE COLUMN COMBINATIONS

A *unique column combination* (UCC) $X$ is a set of attributes $X \subseteq R$ whose projection contains no duplicates in a given relational instance $r$ [Lucchesi and Osborn, 1978]. Unique column combinations, or *uniques* for short, are formally defined as follows [Abedjan and Naumann, 2011].

**Definition 4.2   Unique column combination.**   Given a relational instance $r$ of schema $R$, a *unique column combination* $X$ with $X \subseteq R$ is *valid* in $r$, iff $\forall t_i, t_j \in r, i \neq j : t_i[X] \neq t_j[X]$.

Every UCC $X$ is also a valid FD, namely $X \rightarrow R \setminus X$. For this reason, UCCs and FDs share various properties. A UCC $X$ is a *generalization* of another UCC $Y$ if $X \subset Y$ and it is a *specialization* if $X \supset Y$. Furthermore, if $X$ is a valid UCC, then any $X \cup Z$ with $Z \subseteq R$ is a valid UCC because Armstrong's augmentation rule also applies to UCCs. According to this augmentation rule, a UCC is *minimal* if no attribute $B$ exists such that $X \setminus B$ is still a valid UCC, i.e., if no valid generalization exists. To discover all UCCs in a given relational instance $r$, it suffices to discover all minimal UCCs, because all subsets are non-unique and all supersets are unique by logical inference.

Every unique column combination indicates a syntactically valid key. For example, time-stamps uniquely identify readings from a sensor, IP-addresses identify computers in a network, and geo-coordinates identify buildings. Although UCCs and keys are technically the same, we usually make the distinction that keys are UCCs with semantic meaning, i.e., they hold not only by chance in a relational instance but they hold in all instances of the given schema for a semantic reason [Abedjan et al., 2015b].

Since every valid UCC is also a valid FD, functional dependencies generalize unique column combinations. However, we consider these two types of dependencies separately for the following reasons.

1. *Non-trivial inference*: A minimal UCC is not necessarily the left-hand side of a minimal FD because UCCs are minimal w.r.t. $R$ and FDs are minimal w.r.t. some $A \in R$. For instance, if $X$ is a minimal UCC, then $X \rightarrow R$ is a valid FD and no $Y \subset X$ exists such that $X \setminus Y \rightarrow R$ is still valid. However, $X \setminus Y \rightarrow A$ with $A \in R$ can still be a valid and minimal FD. For this reason, not all minimal UCCs can be directly inferred from the set of minimal FDs; to infer all minimal UCCs, one must systematically specialize the FDs, check if these specializations determine $R$, and if they do, check whether they are minimal w.r.t. $R$.

2. *Duplicate row problem*: The FD $X \rightarrow R \setminus X$ does not necessarily define a UCC $X$ if the given relational instance contains duplicate records. A duplicate record invalidates all possible UCCs because it creates a duplicate value in every attribute and attribute combination. However, a duplicate record does not invalidate any FD because an FD can be invalidated only through two records having different Rhs values. In practice, duplicate

records can occur in join tables, log data, streaming data, and un-managed file formats, such as CSV, which cannot ensure their absence.

3. *Discovery advantage*: UCCs can be discovered more efficiently than FDs because UCCs are easier to verify and the search space is—as we will see in Section 4.2—much smaller. Thus, if a data scientist or IT professional requires only UCCs, discovering FDs is unnecessary.

### 4.1.3 INCLUSION DEPENDENCIES

An *inclusion dependency* (IND) $R_i[X] \subseteq R_j[Y]$ over the relational schemata $R_i$ and $R_j$ states that all values in $X$ also occur in $Y$ [Casanova et al., 1982]. We write $X \subseteq Y$ instead of $R_i[X] \subseteq R_j[Y]$ if it is clear from the context that $X \subseteq Y$ denotes an IND (and not a set inclusion relationship). Inclusion dependencies are formally defined as follows [Marchi et al., 2009].

**Definition 4.3 Inclusion dependency.** Given two relational instances $r_i$ and $r_j$ of schemata $R_i$, and $R_j$, respectively, the *inclusion dependency* $R_i[X] \subseteq R_j[Y]$ (abbreviated $X \subseteq Y$) with attribute list $X \subseteq R_i$, attribute list $Y \subseteq R_j$, and cardinalities $|X| = |Y|$ is *valid* iff $\forall t_i \in r_i, \exists t_j \in r_j : t_i[X] = t_j[Y]$.

Note that $X$ and $Y$ denote attribute *lists* for INDs, i.e., their attribute order may differ from the attribute order in $R$ and they may contain repeated attributes. We call the dependent part $X$ of an IND the *left-hand side*, short LHS, and the referenced part $Y$ the *right hand side*, short RHS.

Suppose we are given two INDs, $X \subseteq Y$ and $X' \subseteq Y'$, with LHS attributes $X = A_1, ..., A_n$ and RHS $Y = B_1, ..., B_n$. If $X' = X \setminus A_i, ..., A_j$ and $Y' = Y \setminus B_i, ..., B_j$, i.e., if $X' \subseteq Y'$ is derivable from $X \subseteq Y$ by removing attributes with the same indices from the lists $X$ and $Y$, then $X \subseteq Y$ is *specialization* of $X' \subseteq Y'$ and, vice versa, $X' \subseteq Y'$ is a *generalization* of $X \subseteq Y$. The *size* or *arity n* of an IND is defined by $n = |X| = |Y|$. We call INDs with $n = 1$ *unary* inclusion dependencies and INDs with $n > 1$ *n-ary* inclusion dependencies. A sound and complete axiomatization for INDs is given by the following three inference rules on schemata $R_i$, $R_j$, and $R_k$ [Casanova et al., 1982].

1. *Reflexivity*: If $i = j$ and $X = Y$ then $R_i[X] \subseteq R_j[Y]$.

2. *Permutation*: If $R_i[A_1, ..., A_n] \subseteq R_j[B_1, ..., B_n]$ then $R_i[A_{\sigma 1}, ..., A_{\sigma m}] \subseteq R_j[B_{\sigma 1}, ..., B_{\sigma m}]$ for each sequence $\sigma 1, ..., \sigma m$ of distinct integers from $\{1, ..., m\}$.

3. *Transitivity*: If $R_i[X] \subseteq R_j[Y]$ and $R_j[Y] \subseteq R_k[Z]$ then $R_i[X] \subseteq R_k[Z]$.

For any $i$ and $X$, an IND $R_i[X] \subseteq R_i[X]$ is said to be *trivial*, as it is always valid according to the reflexivity rule. For valid INDs, all generalizations are also valid INDs, i.e., if $R_i[X] \subseteq R_j[Y]$ is valid, then $R_i[X \setminus A_k] \subseteq R_j[Y \setminus B_k]$ with same attribute indices $k$, $A_k \in X$, and $B_k \in Y$ is valid as well [Marchi et al., 2009]. However, specializations of a valid IND can be valid or invalid. An IND $R_i[X] \subseteq R_j[Y]$ is called *maximal* iff $R_i[XA] \subseteq R_j[YB]$ is *invalid* for all attributes $A \in R_i$ and $B \in R_j$ whose unary inclusion $R_i[A] \subseteq R_j[B]$ is not a generalization of $R_i[X] \subseteq R_j[Y]$. If $R_i[A] \subseteq R_j[B]$ is a generalization, then adding it to $R_i[X] \subseteq R_j[Y]$ always results in a valid IND, but the mapping of $A$ to $B$ would be *redundant* and, therefore, superfluous—the maximal IND would, in a sense, not be minimal. To discover all INDs of a given relational instance $r$, it therefore suffices to discover all maximal, non-trivial INDs.

Usually, we are interested in inclusion dependencies *between different* relations $R_i$ and $R_j$ because these INDs indicate foreign key relationships. However, inclusion dependencies over the same schema are also interesting for data exploration, integrity checking, and query optimization. Consider, for example, a schema Person(id, name, lastname, birthdate, father, mother) that models a family tree. Here, we should find that all values of the attribute father and mother, respectively, are included in the id attribute. From these two INDs we learn that all parents are persons and we can optimize SQL queries accordingly.

## 4.2   SEARCH SPACE AND DATA STRUCTURES

With the understanding of unique column combinations, functional dependencies, and inclusion dependencies that we developed in the previous section, we now discuss how to discover them from data. The discovery of multi-column metadata is a search problem with two dimensions: the number of attributes and the number of records. In this section, we first investigate the attribute dimension by modeling the search space as an attribute lattice. Next, we address the record dimension by discussing position list indices and their applications. The two dimensions lead to a discussion of the complexity of UCC, FD, and IND discovery. We end this section with a discussion of incomplete data, i.e., null values.

### 4.2.1   LATTICES AND SEARCH SPACE SIZES

Dependency discovery algorithms find *all minimal, non-trivial* unique column combinations, *all minimal, non-trivial* functional dependencies, or *all maximal, non-trivial* inclusion dependencies. The search space for these three discovery tasks can be modeled as a graph labeling problem—in fact, the search space of most multi-column dependencies is modeled this way. The basis of this model is a *power set* of attribute combinations [Devlin, 1979]; every possible combination of attributes represents one set. This is a *partially ordered set* because reflexivity, antisymmetry and transitivity hold between the attribute combinations [Deshpande, 1968]. Due to the partial order, every two elements have a unique supremum and a unique infimum. Hence, we can model the partially ordered set as a *lattice*, i.e., a graph of attribute combination nodes that connects each node $X \subseteq R$ to its direct subsets $X \setminus A$ and direct supersets $X \cup B$ (with $A \in X$, $B \in R$ and $B \notin X$). For more details on lattice theory, we refer the reader to Crawley and Dilworth [1973].

A useful visualization of such lattices are Hasse diagrams [Birkhoff, 1940]. Figure 4.1I shows a Hasse diagram for an example relation $R(A, B, C, D, E)$. Note that we did not include

$X = \emptyset$ as a node because $\emptyset$ is neither a valid UCC candidate nor is $\emptyset \subseteq Y$ a valid IND candidate for any $Y \subseteq R$. However, a *functional dependency* candidate $\emptyset \rightarrow Y$ is possible and valid if the column $Y$ is constant, i.e., it contains only one value. Thus, FD discovery algorithms should consider $\emptyset$ in the lattice as well.

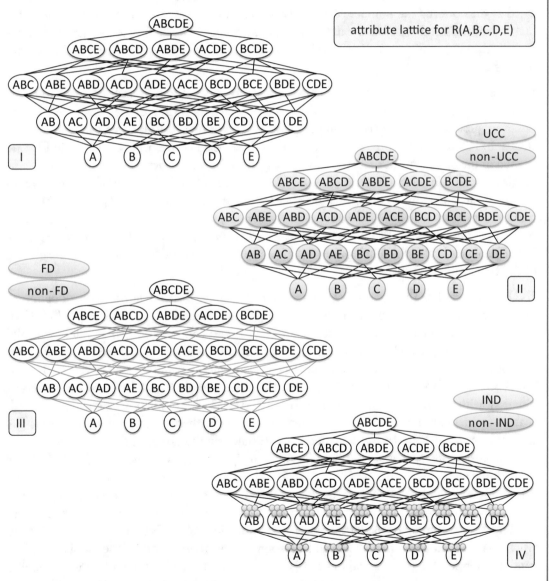

Figure 4.1: The search spaces of UCCs, FDs, and INDs visualized as lattices.

We now map the search space of UCCs, FDs, and INDs to the lattice of attribute combinations.

**UCC discovery:** For UCC discovery, each *node X* represents one UCC candidate, i.e., an attribute combination that is either unique or non-unique with respect to a given relational instance. Figure 4.1II shows a result of a UCC discovery process, with uniques and non-uniques colored differently. UCCs are located in the upper part of the lattice while non-UCCs are located at the bottom. The number of UCC candidates in level $k$ for $m$ attributes is $\binom{m}{k}$, which makes the total number of UCC candidates for $m$ attributes $\sum_{k=1}^{m} \binom{m}{k} = 2^m - 1$. Figure 4.2 visualizes the exponential growth of the UCC candidate search space with respect to the number of attributes.

**FD discovery:** For FD discovery, we map each *edge* between nodes $X$ and $XA$ to an FD candidate $X \to A$. This mapping ensures that only non-trivial candidates are considered. In the discovery process, we classify edges in the graph as valid or invalid FDs in a given relational instance. In Figure 4.1III, we give an example of an FD labeled lattice. Like UCCs, valid FDs are located in the upper part of the lattice and non-FDs in the lower part. The number of FD candidates in level $k$ for $m$ attributes is $\binom{m}{k} \cdot (m - k)$ where $m - k$ is the number of upward edges of a node in the lattice; the total number of FD candidates is therefore $\sum_{k=1}^{m} \binom{m}{k} \cdot (m - k)$. Note that the sum starts with $k = 0$ if we consider $\emptyset$ as a node; then, the number of FD candidates is $\sum_{k=0}^{m} \binom{m}{k} \cdot (m - k) \leq \frac{m}{2} \cdot 2^m$. The growth of the FD candidate space with respect to the number of attributes is visualized in Figure 4.2. It is also exponential and even faster than the growth of the UCC candidate space.

**IND discovery:** For IND discovery, we annotate each node $X$ in the lattice with all permutations of attribute sets $Y$ of the same size, i.e., all permutations of $Y \subset R$ with $|Y| = |X|$. Each such *annotation* represents an IND candidate $X \subseteq Y$ and can be classified as valid or invalid with respect to a given relational instance. These annotations also include trivial combinations, such as $A \subseteq A$ and $X \subseteq X$, and combinations with repeated attributes, such as $AA \subseteq BC$ and $ABC \subseteq BCB$. However, most IND discovery algorithms ignore trivial combinations and combinations with duplicates. Even without these ignored INDs, the number of candidates is so high that we restrict our visualization of the search space even further: we consider only those INDs $X \subseteq Y$ where $Y \cap X = \emptyset$, i.e., the dependent attributes should not overlap with the referenced attributes—a property that should hold for most foreign-key constraints. Most IND discovery algorithms make this restriction [Liu et al., 2012], although it is not required for correctness. The example in Figure 4.1IV shows that due to $Y \cap X = \emptyset$, the annotations exist only up to level $\lfloor \frac{m}{2} \rfloor$. It also shows that, in contrast to UCCs and FDs, valid INDs are located at the *bottom* and invalid INDs at the top of the lattice—as stated in Section 4.1.3, INDs might become invalid when adding attributes while UCCs and FDs remain (or become) valid. The number of IND candidates in level $k$ for $m$ attributes is $\binom{m}{k} \cdot \binom{m-k}{k} \cdot k!$, where $\binom{m-k}{k}$ are all non-overlapping attribute sets of a lattice node and $k!$ all permutations of such a non-overlapping attribute set.

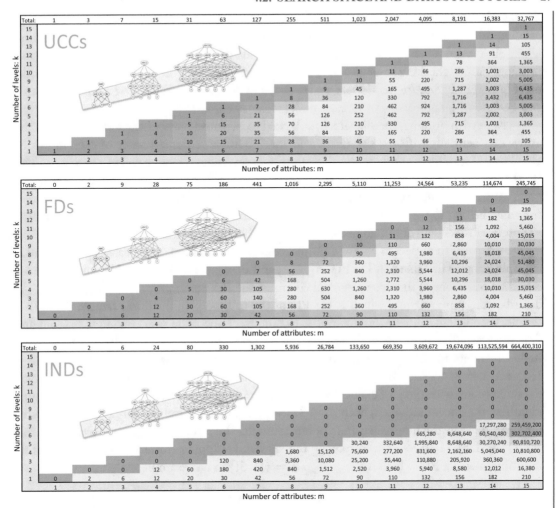

Figure 4.2: Search space sizes for UCCs, FDs, and INDs.

Thus, the total number of IND candidates is $\sum_{k=1}^{m} \binom{m}{k} \cdot \binom{m-k}{k} \cdot k!$. Figure 4.2 shows that this number is much larger than the number of UCC or FD candidates given the same number of attributes, although IND candidates reach to only half the lattice height.

## 4.2.2 POSITION LIST INDEXES AND SEARCH SPACE VALIDATION

Discovering UCCs, FDs, and INDs involves data preparation, search space traversal, candidate generation, and candidate checking. Candidate checking is the most expensive step for most profiling algorithms, because the checks are executed often and operate on instance-level (and not on schema-level). This motivates the use of the inference rules discussed in Section 4.1 as pruning rules to avoid as many of these checks as possible. For instance, if $X$ was identified as a UCC, all $X'$ with $X' \supset X$ must also be valid UCCs and do not have to be checked. To maximize pruning, various checking strategies have been proposed based on the lattice search space model, most importantly *breadth-first bottom-up* [Huhtala et al., 1999], *breadth-first top-down* [Marchi and Petit, 2003], and *depth-first random walk* [Heise et al., 2013].

Even with pruning, the algorithms still need to execute a number of candidate checks that grows exponentially with the size of the schema. To improve the efficiency of each individual UCC or FD candidate check, many algorithms rely on a data structure called *position list index* (PLI), which is also known as *stripped partitions* [Cosmadakis et al., 1986]. A PLI, denoted by $\pi_X$, groups tuples into equivalence classes or clusters by their values of an attribute set $X$. Two tuples, $t_1$ and $t_2$, belong to the same equivalence class with respect to $X$ if $\forall A \in X : t_1[A] = t_2[A]$. A PLI omits clusters with only a single entry, meaning that tuples that do not occur in any cluster of $\pi_X$ are unique with respect to $X$. For example, consider the relation Class(Teacher, Subject) and its example instance in Table 4.2. The PLIs $\pi_{\{Teacher\}}$ and $\pi_{\{Subject\}}$, which are also shown in Table 4.2, represent partitions of the two individual columns; the PLI $\pi_{\{Teacher, Subject\}} = \pi_{\{Teacher\}} \cap \pi_{\{Subject\}}$ describes their intersection, which is the PLI of the column combination $\{Teacher, Subject\}$. A simple, yet efficient, implementation of the PLI intersect operation takes two PLIs as input and, first, inverts one of them, the probing-side, into an inverted index, i.e., one that points the PLI's tuple identifiers to their partition indices. For example, $\pi_{\{Subject\}}$ would become $\{1 \rightarrow 1, 2 \rightarrow 1, 5 \rightarrow 1, 3 \rightarrow 2, 4 \rightarrow 2\}$. Then, the operation scans the other PLI, the build-side, to calculate the intersection with the probe-side. With the inverted index, it quickly obtains, for every tuple identifier, the cluster indices in both PLIs. These pairs of cluster indices define the new clusters for every tuple in the intersected PLI. In our example, the result for $\pi_{\{Teacher\}} \cap \pi_{\{Subject\}}$ is thus $\{(1, 1) \rightarrow \{1, 5\}, (1, 2) \rightarrow \{3\}\}$. Removing the keys and stripping clusters of size one yields the resulting intersect PLI, which is $\pi_{\{Teacher, Subject\}} = \{\{1, 5\}\}$ in our example.

Table 4.2: An example instance for the schema Class(Teacher, Subject) and its PLIs

|  | Teacher | Subject |
|---|---------|---------|
| $t_1$ | Brown | Math |
| $t_2$ | Walker | Math |
| $t_3$ | Brown | English |
| $t_4$ | Miller | English |
| $t_5$ | Brown | Math |

$$\pi\{Teacher\} = \{\{1, 3, 5\}\}$$
$$\pi\{Subject\} = \{\{1, 2, 5\}, \{3, 4\}\}$$
$$\pi\{Teacher,\ Subject\} = \{\{1,5\}\}$$

$X$ is a unique column combination iff $\pi_X$ does not contain any clusters (of size greater than one) and therefore no value combination in $X$ occurs more than once. To check a functional dependency $X \rightarrow A$, we test if every cluster in $\pi_X$ is a subset of some cluster in $\pi_A$, i.e., if $\pi_X \cap \pi_A = \pi_X$. If so, then all tuples with same values in $X$ have also same values in $A$. This check is called *refinement* and was first introduced in Huhtala et al. [1999]. It can be implemented as a simple PLI intersection (see above) or optimized variants of this operation (see for instance Section 4.4.8).

### 4.2.3    SEARCH COMPLEXITY

Despite their practical importance, pruning rules and position list indices do not change the complexity of dependency discovery. Beeri et al. showed that the following problem is NP-complete [Beeri et al., 1984]: given a relation schema and an integer $i > 1$, decide whether there exists a key of cardinality less than $i$. Thus, finding *one* key or unique column combination is already an NP-complete problem. The same also holds for functional dependencies [Davies and Russell, 1994] and inclusion dependencies [Kantola et al., 1992]. Therefore, the discovery of *all minimal/maximal* UCCs, FDs, and INDs is NP-hard. Solutions to these discovery problems are exponential in the number attributes $m$, and, if nested loop joins are used for candidate validation, quadratic in the number of records $n$. More specifically, UCC discovery is in $\mathcal{O}(n^2 \cdot 2^m)$, FD discovery is in $\mathcal{O}(n^2 \cdot 2^m \cdot (\frac{m}{2})^2)$, and IND discovery is in $\mathcal{O}(n^2 \cdot 2^m \cdot m!)$, with $m!$ being a simplification [Liu et al., 2012]. This makes UCC discovery the easiest of the three tasks and IND discovery the most difficult one. Note that $n^2$ is an upper bound for all discovery problems and can be improved using, for instance, sorting- or hashing-based candidate validation techniques.

The complexity of dependency discovery is exponential because the solution size can grow exponentially in the number of attributes [Gunopulos et al., 2003]. This means that if we have an oracle algorithm that validates only the true dependencies of a given dataset, it would still need to test an exponentially growing set of candidates. For instance, the worst case number of minimal unique column combinations is $\binom{|R|}{\frac{|R|}{2}} \geq 2^{\frac{|R|}{2}}$ because all combinations of size $\frac{|R|}{2}$ can simultaneously be minimal uniques.

Some NP-complete problems can be easier to solve than others, as we often find parameters $k$ that cause the exponential complexity while the rest of the algorithm is polynomial in the size of the input $n$. More formally, we may find an algorithm that runs in $\mathcal{O}(f(k) \cdot p(n))$ time with an exponential function $f$ and a polynomial function $p$ [Downey and Fellows, 1999]. If such an algorithm exists for an NP-complete problem, the problem is called *fixed-parameter tractable* (FPT). An FPT solution to an NP-complete problem is efficient if the parameter $k$ is small (or even fixed) due to some practical assumption. For key dependencies, $k$ could, for instance, be the maximum size of a dependency—a parameter that we can easily enforce. However, Bläsius et al. showed that our three problems do *not* admit FPT algorithms [Bläsius et al., 2017]. Regarding the $W$-hierarchy, which is a classification of computational complexities, they prove that UCC discovery and FD discovery are $W[2]$-complete and IND discovery is $W[3]$-complete. This makes IND discovery one of the hardest natural problems known today; one of the rare other known $W[t]$-complete natural problems with $t > 2$ is related to supply chain management [Chen and Zhang, 2006].

### 4.2.4   NULL SEMANTICS

Datasets are often incomplete, which means that we either do not know the value of a certain attribute or that the attribute does not apply to all entities in the relation. In such cases, null values $\perp$ are used to indicate *no value* [Garcia-Molina et al., 2008]. For the discovery of dependencies, null values may be problematic because the validity of a dependency relies on the existence of values that either support or contradict it.

The standard solution for null values in data profiling is to define the semantics of null comparisons. Expressions of the form null $= x$ with some value $x$ always evaluate to false because the assumption that the same null value is simultaneously equal to all possible $x$ values leads to inconsistent conclusions. However, the expression null $=$ null either consistently evaluates to true or to false—either we consider all null values to represent the same value or different values.

Deciding between null $=$ null or null $\neq$ null impacts key dependencies. For example, consider the schema $R(A, B)$ with two tuples, $t_1 = (\perp, 1)$ and $t_2 = (\perp, 2)$. Depending on this decision, the UCC $\{A\}$ and the FD $A \rightarrow B$ are both either false or true. When switching the semantics from null $\neq$ null to null $=$ null, minimal UCCs tend to become larger on average because more attributes are needed to make attribute combinations with null values unique. However, minimal FDs can become smaller or larger, i.e., null values in LHS attributes introduce violations that require additional LHS attributes and null values in RHS attributes resolve violations with respect to the LHS attributes. In general, null $=$ null is the *pessimistic* perspective and null $\neq$ null the *optimistic* perspective for key dependencies.

To choose between the two null semantics, one obvious idea is to handle null values as in SQL. In SQL, null $=$ null evaluates to unknown, which is neither true nor false [Garcia-Molina et al., 2008]. In some cases, unknown is effectively treated as false, e.g., null values do not match in join statements. In other cases, unknown is treated as true, e.g., in group-by statements. For this reason, SQL does not help with this decision.

Most discovery algorithms support both null semantics. However, most implementations agree to use the pessimistic null $=$ null semantics in experiments and default configurations for the following two reasons [Papenbrock et al., 2015b]. First, it is believed to be more intuitive because a completely empty column, for instance, should not functionally determine all other columns; second, it is more challenging because many null-affected dependencies are located in higher lattice levels.

Note that an agreement on null semantics is a simplification of the null problem. A precise interpretation of a null value is *no information* [Zaniolo, 1984], which was first introduced for functional dependencies and constraints in Atzeni and Morfuni [1986]. Köhler and Link derived two validity models for this null interpretation, namely the *possible world* model and the *certain world* model. A dependency is valid in the possible world model iff at least *one* replacement of all null values exists that satisfies the dependency; the dependency is valid in the certain world model iff *every* replacement of the null values satisfies the dependency [Köhler and Link, 2016, Köhler et al., 2015]. To ensure possible and certain world validity, discovery algorithms require additional reasoning about null replacements, which most algorithms omit due to the associated complexity. For more details on possible and certain world key dependencies, we refer the reader to Le et al. [2015].

## 4.3    DISCOVERING UNIQUE COLUMN COMBINATIONS

In the literature, we find two classes of discovery algorithms for unique column combinations: *column-based* approaches that systematically validate one UCC candidate after another and *row-based* approaches that derive UCCs from pairwise record comparisons. Both approaches have exponential worst-case complexity, but column-based algorithms have been shown to be more efficient on datasets with many rows (as they avoid comparing all pairs of records) whereas row-based algorithms perform better on datasets with many columns (as they consider fewer candidates) [Abedjan et al., 2014c, Papenbrock et al., 2015b]. We explain the two classes of algorithms below.

**Column-based approaches:** These algorithms model the search space as a lattice of UCC candidates, as discussed in Section 4.2.1. Each node in the lattice represents one UCC candidate. An efficient way of validating a unique column combination is to use PLIs, as discussed in Section 4.2.2: $X$ is a valid UCC iff the $\pi_X$ does not contain any clusters. This strategy is used by column-based algorithms such as HCA [Abedjan and Naumann, 2011], DUCC [Heise et al., 2013], and SWAN [Abedjan et al., 2014b]. What distinguishes these algorithms from each other is the order in which they traverse the lattice. The *breadth-first bottom-up* strategy used in HCA starts with "small" UCC candidates (in terms of the number of attributes) and works its way to larger candidates, i.e., from the bottom of the lattice to the top. The *breadth-first top-down* starts at the top of the lattice and traverses down to the bottom. The *depth-first random-walk* strategy of DUCC starts with one candidate at the bottom of the lattice and performs a random-walk where the next step depends on the result of the previous candidate validation. All three strategies make use of superset- and subset-pruning rules for UCCs. Column-based discovery algorithms are also referred to as *top-down* approaches, which should not be confused with top-down lattice traversal. For clarity, we will refer to these algorithms only as *column-based* or *lattice traversal* algorithms.

**Row-based approaches:** These types of algorithms, such as GORDIAN [Sismanis et al., 2006], compare pairs of records in the dataset, derive non-uniques, i.e., non-valid UCCs, and finally derive all minimal UCCs from the non-uniques. Row-based approaches do not explicitly create UCC candidates—an advantage over column-based approaches because the number of candidates can be very large. Row-based discovery algorithms are also known as *bottom-up* approaches, where "bottom" denotes the records (as opposed to "top" denoting the attributes), which, again, can be confused with bottom-up lattice traversal. For clarity, we refer to this class of algorithms as *row-based* or *dependency induction* algorithms.

Since both column- and row-based algorithms have their strengths, hybrid discovery approaches have been proposed to combine both search strategies. HYUCC [Papenbrock and Naumann, 2017a] is one such algorithm that discovers UCCs by alternating between comparing records and checking candidates. This is more efficient than the two individual search strategies, but one must understand both classes of algorithms to implement their combination. Thus, we discuss all five UCC discovery algorithms, i.e., GORDIAN, HCA, DUCC, SWAN, and HYUCC, in the remainder of this section.

### 4.3.1 GORDIAN

GORDIAN [Sismanis et al., 2006] is a row-based UCC discovery algorithm that benefits from the observation that *non-uniques* can be detected without considering every row of the given dataset. To determine the *validity* of a UCC $X$, one needs to consider the values of all tuples $t_i[X]$ and check that they are unique; in contrast, to determine the *invalidity* of a UCC $X$, one needs to find only two tuples $t_1$ and $t_2$ with $t_1[X] = t_2[X]$. For example in Table 4.3, scanning the *age* column can be stopped right after the second occurence of the value 24 has been discovered. Once all non-uniques are discovered—all *maximal* non-uniques are, in fact, sufficient—GORDIAN can infer all valid minimal UCCs from them. The overall algorithm consists of three parts: (i) organize the data in a prefix tree, (ii) find maximal non-uniques by traversing the prefix tree, and (iii) compute minimal uniques from maximal non-uniques.

Table 4.3: Example dataset

| Tuple ID | First | Last | Age | Phone |
|----------|-------|-------|-----|-------|
| 1 | Max | Payne | 32 | 1234 |
| 2 | Eve | Smith | 24 | 5432 |
| 3 | Eve | Payne | 24 | 3333 |
| 4 | Max | Payne | 24 | 3333 |

GORDIAN stores the prefix tree in memory. Each level of the tree represents one column whereas each branch corresponds to one distinct tuple. Tuples that have the same values in their prefix share the corresponding branches. Figure 4.3 shows the prefix tree corresponding to our running example. The numbers at each node represent the order of node creation. There are fewer nodes than cells in the table as common prefixes of tuples are merged when possible. Each branch of the tree has a counter that is typically less than 2, denoting the number of tuples that are represented by the branch. A number higher than 1 would denote a duplicate record.

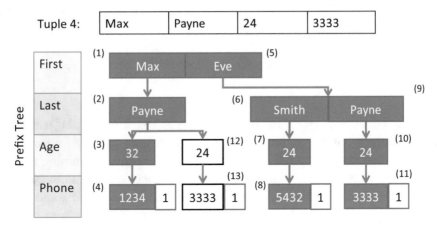

Figure 4.3: Inserting the fourth tuple from Table 4.3 into the prefix tree.

The time to create the prefix tree depends on the number of rows, meaning that it can be a bottleneck for very large datasets. Tree traversal is based on the data cube operator [Gray et al., 1997], which computes aggregate functions on projected columns. With the cube operator, non-unique discovery is performed by a depth-first traversal of the tree that searches for maximum repeated branches, which constitute maximal non-uniques. For example the algorithm would project our slices from each branch and check whether the nodes are singletons or have pointers to more than one child node. In our example, the column combination {*first,last*} would be marked as a non-unique as the path from *Max* to *Payne* points to two different child nodes, indicating duplicate values.

After discovering all maximal non-uniques, GORDIAN computes all minimal uniques by generating minimal combinations that are not covered by any of the maximal non-uniques, i.e., the complement set of maximal non-uniques. In our running example, the set of maximal non-uniques is {{*first,last*}, {*last,age,phone*}, {*first,age*}}. The set of minimal uniques is therefore {{*first,last,age*}, {*first,phone*}}. In Sismanis et al. [2006], it is stated that this step has quadratic complexity in the number of minimal uniques, but the presented algorithm implies cubic runtime: for each non-unique, the updated set of minimal uniques needs to be *simplified* by removing redundant uniques. This simplification requires quadratic runtime in the number of uniques. As the number of minimal uniques is bounded linearly by the number $s$ of maximal non-uniques, the runtime of the unique generation step is $O(s^3)$.

GORDIAN exploits the fact that non-uniques can be discovered faster than uniques, i.e., that non-uniques can be marked as such as soon as one repeated value is discovered. Converting the data into a prefix structure facilitates this analysis. It is stated that the algorithm is polynomial in the number of tuples for data with a Zipfian distribution of values. In the worst case, however, GORDIAN takes exponential runtime.

The generation of minimal uniques from maximal non-uniques can be a bottleneck if there are many maximal non-uniques. Experiments showed that in most cases, the runtime is dominated by unique generation [Abedjan and Naumann, 2011]. GORDIAN also has a relatively high memory consumption because the prefix tree does not compress the data as tightly as PLIs.

### 4.3.2   HCA

The column-based discovery algorithm HCA [Abedjan and Naumann, 2011] uses PLIs for candidate validation and a bottom-up breadth-first lattice traversal strategy for candidate generation. The lattice traversal is inspired by the *apriori-gen* algorithm for mining frequent itemsets [Agrawal and Srikant, 1994]. To identify frequent itemsets, or, in this case, unique column combinations, in lattice level $k$, the algorithm considers all column combinations in lattice level $k - 1$. It then outputs all those column combinations $X$ with $|X| = k$ as new candidates that have no valid subset, i.e., where all $X' \subset X$ with $|X| = k - 1$ are invalid UCCs; if at least one $X'$ is valid, $X$ must also be valid but not minimal (minimality pruning). The effectiveness and theoretical background of *apriori-gen* based algorithms is discussed in detail by Giannella and Wyss [1999]. The authors present three breadth-first traversal strategies: bottom-up, top-down, and hybrid traversal. For more in-depth details on these strategies, we refer the reader to their publication.

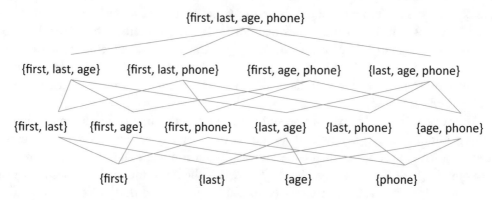

Figure 4.4: Powerset lattice for the example dataset in Table 4.3.

We now return to the HCA algorithm and its candidate generation. Assume that we run the algorithm over Table 4.3. HCA traverses the lattice shown in Figure 4.4, beginning with all 1-*combinations*, i.e., attribute sets of size one (the same applies for *k-candidates*, *k-uniques*, and *k-non-uniques*). Each 1-*combination* can be considered a *1-candidate*, i.e., it is selected for verification. To generate *2-candidates*, the algorithm generates all pairs of *1-non-uniques*. All *k*-candidates with $k > 2$ are generated by combining two $(k - 1)$-*non-uniques* that share the same $(k - 2)$-long prefix. The algorithm later checks whether each candidate consists of only non-unique subset combinations and removes those that do not. After candidate generation, the actual content of each candidate is checked to verify its uniqueness. If the candidate is non-unique, HCA adds the *k-candidate* to the list of *k-non-uniques*; otherwise it is unique and its minimality has to be checked before being added to the result set. HCA terminates when $k = |1\text{-}non\text{-}uniques|$, which can be much earlier than the last level of the lattice.

The *apriori-gen* idea can also be applied to the top-down and hybrid lattice traversal strategies. Given a set of *k-uniques*, top-down traversal checks whether these *k-uniques* are minimal. For this purpose, top-down traversal generates and validates all $(k-1)$-*subsets* for each *k-unique*. If all these subsets are invalid for one specific *k-unique*, this *k-unique* is minimal. Hybrid traversal generates the $k$th and $(n-k)$th levels simultaneously. It then uses bottom-up generation rules for level $k$ and top-down generation rules for level $(n-k)$. Experiments have shown that in most datasets, uniques usually occur in lower levels of the lattice, which favors bottom-up traversal [Abedjan and Naumann, 2011].

The HCA algorithm optimizes the candidate validation step by applying additional statistical pruning, i.e., the algorithm also considers value histograms and distinct counts before testing a UCC candidate via PLI intersection. These statistics can be retrieved on the fly from previous levels during lattice traversal. To illustrate statistics-based pruning, consider the *1-non-uniques* last and age from Table 4.3. The column combination {last,age} cannot be unique based on the value distributions. While the value "Payne" occurs three times in last, the column age contains only two distinct values. That means at least two of the rows containing the value "Payne" also have a duplicate value in the age column. Using the count distinct values, HCA also detects some functional dependencies on the fly and leverages them to avoid unnecessary uniqueness checks.

In contrast to GORDIAN, HCA avoids comparing all record pairs, which is why the algorithm performs well for datasets with a large number of records. However, lattice traversal becomes inefficient if the number of attributes grows because the number of minimal UCCs grows exponentially and their average height in the lattice moves upward, which causes HCA to inspect an exponentially growing number of non-UCCs. We visualized this growth in Section 4.2.1.

### 4.3.3  DUCC

The DUCC algorithm [Heise et al., 2013] is another column-based approach. In contrast to HCA, DUCC uses a depth-first random-walk lattice traversal strategy for candidate generation. Depth-first traversal allows DUCC to prune not only upward, i.e., generalizations of known UCCs that must be true as well (minimality pruning), but also prune downward, i.e., specializations of known non-UCCs that must be false (invalidity pruning). Downward pruning, in particular, can significantly reduce the number of non-UCCs that breadth-first approaches need to check if the valid UCCs are located in higher lattice levels. In our running example, the minimal unique {*first,last,age*} can only be verified if all of its six subsets have been checked.

Depth-first random-walk candidate generation resembles the problem of identifying the most promising paths through the lattice to discover minimal uniques and avoid unnecessary uniqueness checks. The intuition is that minimal UCCs are arranged in the lattice like pearls on a string. That is, we find non-uniques at the bottom of the lattice, uniques at the top, and minimal uniques, which are uniques that UCC discovery algorithms aim to find, on a virtual border between uniques and non-uniques. Ducc tries to reach this virtual border as quickly as possible (depth-first); then, it traverses the border between uniques and non-uniques, maximizing the effect of upward and downward pruning.

Considering all bottom-level UCC candidates as starting points for lattice traversal, Ducc's random walk proceeds as follows. First, it starts with one such candidate, e.g., column *first*. If the candidate is a valid UCC, it moves on to another randomly selected bottom-level candidate; otherwise, it proceeds to a random specialization of the non-UCC in the second level. As soon as the walk has left the bottom level, each further step is defined by the validity of the current candidate. If the candidate is valid, we prune all specializations and choose a random, yet unclassified generalization of it by removing an attribute from the candidate (go down in the lattice); if the candidate is invalid, we prune all generalizations and choose a random, yet unclassified specialization of it by adding a new attribute to the candidate (go up in the lattice). In our example, *first* is not a unique, so it will be randomly combined with a different column, e.g., *last*. As the combination {*first,last*} is still non-unique, we mark *last* as unique as well and we move up the lattice to the next level. If the combination {*first,last,age*} is then selected, it would be verified to be unique and we can omit its supersets. Now the algorithm would randomly pick an unclassified subset, such as {*first,age*}. If the algorithm does not find an unclassified generalization or specialization, it backtracks to the original candidate.

The walk ends if it cannot reach any further unclassified candidates. At that point, the lattice might still contain "islands" of unclassified UCC candidates that are not reachable by any branch of the path traversed so far. Such holes in the search space arise from the combination of upward and downward pruning, which might cut off areas from the search. In order to detect and validate such missing candidates, Ducc proposes a hole finding post-processing step that complements the discovered maximum non-uniques, similar to the GORDIAN algorithm, and checks them against the discovered minimal uniques. All nodes in the complement set must be valid uniques, i.e., they must be known minimal uniques or supersets of them; otherwise, they are unclassified candidates and serve as new seeds for further random walks. For the algorithm to work correctly, Ducc remembers which candidates are valid and which are not, and it must determine whether valid UCCs are *minimal* and invalid UCCs are *maximal*.

For candidate validation, Ducc uses PLIs and the PLI intersection operation. To obtain the PLI of a column combination, Ducc identifies the PLI of the next smaller subsets and intersects them. If the walk is upward, this is simply the last PLI with the unary PLI of the added attribute; otherwise, if the walk is downward, the algorithm must search for the PLI of the largest subset. For this reason, Ducc maintains all PLIs in a cache for later re-use.

Experiments on Ducc in Heise et al. [2013] have shown that the algorithm performs significantly better than HCA and better than Gordian. In addition to the random walk, the authors also proposed a parallel, distributed application of Ducc for better scalability. Here, multiple workers pursue different random walks in parallel, which can fill holes in the search space.

### 4.3.4   HYUCC

Since both column- and row-based discovery approaches have their strengths, HyUCC [Papenbrock and Naumann, 2017a] combines both search strategies into one hybrid algorithm. The idea is to automatically switch back and forth between the two strategies depending on which strategy currently performs better. The two challenges for these switches are, first, to decide when to switch and, second, to transfer intermediate results from one phase to the other. To understand how HyUCC solves these challenges, we first briefly discuss the two individual discovery strategies and then their hybrid combination.

**Row-based strategy:** The row-based UCC discovery strategy compares records pairwise and derives the so-called agree sets from these comparisons. An agree set is a set of attributes that have the same values in the two compared records and therefore cannot be a UCC. Thus, agree sets directly correspond to non-UCCs in the attribute lattice. Similar to the Gordian algorithm and an algorithm called Fdep in Flach and Savnik [1999], these non-UCCs can be turned into true UCCs.

Since comparing all pairs of records is expensive, HyUCC only compares records from a sample, $r'$, of $r$. When converting the discovered agree sets into minimal UCCs, these $r'$-UCCs are unique in the sample $r'$ but may not be unique in all of $r$. Nevertheless, $r'$-UCC sets have three useful properties. First, they are *complete* because they contain or imply (as supersets of $r'$-UCCs) all the true UCCs that hold in all of $r$. Second, they are *minimal* because all minimal $r'$-UCCs are also minimal $r$-UCCs if they are true UCCs in all of $r$, or they imply minimal $r$-UCCs as their supersets if they do not hold in all of $r$. Third, $r'$-UCC sets are *proximal*, which means that $r'$-UCCs are closer to the true $r$-UCCs (in terms of the number of attributes) than unary UCC candidates at the bottom of the lattice.

For maximum pruning, HyUCC focuses on record pairs that are more likely to produce new UCC violations. The proposed way of achieving this is to utilize the pre-calculated position list indexes that group records with similar values into clusters. Intuitively, records that share no cluster cannot produce violations and do not need to be compared; records that share many clusters produce large agree sets that invalidate many candidates at once, which is why they should be compared first. This strategy is called *focused sampling* and helps to quickly exclude many UCC candidates at the bottom of the lattice.

**Column-based strategy:** For a column-based search, HyUCC proposes a simple bottom-up breadth-first lattice traversal strategy similar to the HCA algorithm. First, it tests all candidates of size one, then of size two and so on. During the traversal, minimality pruning ensures that candidates are generated only for potentially minimal UCCs. The candidates in a given lattice level can be validated in parallel because they are independent of one another.

In contrast to HCA and Ducc, HyUCC always uses single column Plis $\pi_A$, which are calculated initially, for all higher-level candidate validations and does not cache multi-column Plis $\pi_X$. This reduces the algorithm's memory consumption and, because higher-level Plis are not needed later on, allows the algorithm to stop the intersection process of a set of $\pi_A$s as soon as one duplicate value has been found.

**Hybrid strategy:** Here, row-based search is used in the *sampling phase* to inspect carefully chosen subsets of record pairs for agree sets, and column-based search is used in the *validation phase*. HyUCC uses the sampling phase to identify as many non-UCCs as possible and the validation phase to produce a valid result: it starts with the sampling phase, then switches back and forth, and finally ends with the validation phase. The questions that remain are *when* and *how* to switch.

The best time to stop the sampling phase is when most of the non-UCCs have been identified and finding more non-UCCs becomes more expensive than directly validating the candidates. To find the best time, HyUCC switches back and forth whenever a phase becomes *inefficient*. Sampling becomes inefficient when the number of newly discovered agree sets per tuple pair falls below a certain threshold; the validation phase becomes inefficient when the number of valid UCCs per non-UCC falls below a certain threshold. With every switch, the first threshold is relaxed, so that sampling is considered efficient again. This way, the hybrid discovery process always pursues the currently most efficient strategy.

To exchange intermediate results between the two phases, HyUCC maintains all currently valid UCCs in a prefix tree. When the algorithm switches from sampling to validation, it invalidates UCCs for which an agree set was found. When switching from validation to sampling, record pairs that were found to validate many UCC candidates can be used in the sampling phase as they are likely to produce large agree sets. Thus, both phases benefit each other.

Both discovery strategies, i.e., the random walk in Ducc and the hybrid search in HyUCC, reduce the number of validation operations on non-UCCs, either by downward pruning or by selective record comparisons. Thus, both approaches outperform HCA and Gordian. In comparative experiments the hybrid approach was found to be faster and more memory-efficient because the pruning effect of the sampling phase is superior, the pruning does not generate holes, and validations can use early termination [Papenbrock and Naumann, 2017a].

## 4.3.5   SWAN

Swan [Abedjan et al., 2014b] is an incremental discovery algorithm for unique column combinations. The algorithm starts with an initial dataset for which the UCCs are already known (or uses one of the previously discussed discovery algorithms to find them). Swan then maintains the set of UCCs as the dataset changes, i.e., it monitors all inserts and deletes and applies their effect to the set of UCCs. Inserted records may invalidate existing UCCs while removed records may turn non-UCCs into UCCs. The algorithm relies on the observation that most changes to the data will not affect existing UCCs.

To efficiently recognize the effects of inserts and deletes, SWAN maintains a set of indexes over the known minimal uniques and maximal non-uniques. SWAN constructs these indexes based on the initial set of minimal UCCs in a way that avoids a full table scan.

The *Inserts Handler* used in SWAN takes as input a batch of inserted tuples, checks all minimal uniques for uniqueness using the indexes, and updates the sets of minimal uniques and maximal non-uniques if necessary. The overall strategy is to index a minimal set of columns that covers most of the unique column combinations. Minimality is important as index verification can be expensive. Upon insertion, these indexes are checked for possible duplicate values that violate existing UCCs.

Similarly, the *Deletes Handler* takes as input a batch of deleted tuples, searches for duplicates of these tuples in all maximal non-uniques, and updates the results accordingly. The relevant index for this task is the Pli's that have been generated while initially discovering maximal non-uniques and minimal UCCs. Once a record is deleted, its ID will be removed from the existing Pli. Once a Pli shrinks to fewer than two records, there is a chance that some maximal non-uniques might turn into minimal UCCs.

## 4.4 DISCOVERING FUNCTIONAL DEPENDENCIES

Functional dependencies play an important role in many data management use cases, which led to the development of several FD discovery algorithms. We can again classify these algorithms into row- and column-based strategies. Similar to UCC discovery, row-based strategies perform well on datasets with many columns while column-based strategies perform well on datasets with many rows. Since some FD discovery algorithms do not strictly follow this column/row-based classification (they use both types of strategies), we use an alternative, more fine-grained classification for FD discovery:

**Lattice traversal algorithms:** TANE [Huhtala et al., 1999], FUN [Novelli and Cicchetti, 2001], FD_MINE [Yao et al., 2002], and DFD [Abedjan et al., 2014c] are column-based lattice-traversal algorithms. The first three algorithms search through the candidate lattice level-wise bottom-up using the *apriori-gen* candidate generation [Agrawal and Srikant, 1994], whereas DFD applies a depth-first random walk. Lattice traversal algorithms generally use pruning rules to reduce the search space size during FD discovery and their candidate validation is based on position list indexes. They perform well on datasets with many records, but scale poorly with the number of columns due to their candidate-driven search strategy.

**Difference- and agree-set algorithms:** DEP-MINER [Lopes et al., 2000] and FASTFDs [Wyss et al., 2001] search for sets of attributes whose values are the same in at least one tuple pair. These so-called agree-sets are transformed into difference-sets from which all valid FDs can be derived. When computing the agree-sets, the algorithms in this family need to compare the records pairwise. Hence, their discovery strategy is row-based and scales quadratically with the number of records. DEP-MINER [Lopes et al., 2000] and FastFDs [Wyss et al., 2001] also utilize column-based constructs, i.e., position list indexes, to improve the efficiency of the agree-set computation. Since deriving FDs from agree-sets is more efficient than the systematic generation and validation of FD candidates, difference- and agree-set algorithms scale better with the number of attributes than lattice traversal algorithms. The calculation time for the necessary maximization of agree-sets (or minimization of difference-sets) still scales exponentially with the number of attributes.

**Dependency induction algorithms:** The FDEP [Flach and Savnik, 1999] algorithm also compares records pairwise to find all *invalid* functional dependencies. This set is called *negative cover* and is stored in a prefix tree. In contrast to DEP-MINER and FastFDs, FDEP translates the negative cover into the set of valid functional dependencies, i.e., the *positive cover*, not by forming complements but by successive specialization. The positive cover initially assumes that each attribute functionally determines all other attributes; these FDs are then refined using the non-FDs in the negative cover. Apart from the fact that pairwise comparisons do not scale with the number of records, this discovery strategy has proven to scale well with the number of attributes.

**Hybrid algorithms:** Hybrid FD discovery algorithms such as HyFD [Papenbrock and Naumann, 2016] combine independent discovery strategies into a new strategy. The goal is not to identify the most efficient approach for a particular dataset, but to create a new strategy that aims to outperform the individual strategies. The HyFD algorithm achieves this by switching back and forth between lattice traversal and dependency induction.

**Parallel algorithms:** Parallel and distributed dependency discovery systems, such as Garnaud et al. [2014] and Li et al. [2015], rely on massive parallelization rather than pruning. However, parallelization is also applied to algorithms such as ParaDe [Garnaud et al., 2014] and HyFD [Papenbrock and Naumann, 2016], which use it as an additional optimization rather than their main discovery strategy.

All FD profiling algorithms that exists today are in-memory algorithms, i.e., the data are read once, usually compressed into position list indexes, and then used as random-access data structures. Little attention has been payed to disk-backed data structures because the compressed data is relatively small in contrast to the intermediate data structures that most algorithms produce. The result size, which is the size of the set of minimal FDs, also grows exponentially with the number of attributes. Thus, if a profiling algorithm runs out of memory, then this is usually due to their own memory consumption or the size of their output. Since memory issues can also be fought by adding more hardware, most algorithmic approaches to the discovery of FDs try to optimize the discovery time rather than memory consumption. In the remainder of this section, we discuss TANE, FUN, FD_MINE, DFD, DEP-MINER, FASTFDs, FDEP, and HYFD. We note that these algorithms have also been summarized in Papenbrock et al. [2015b].

### 4.4.1 TANE

The TANE algorithm by Huhtala et al. [1999] is based on three main concepts: *partition refinement* via PLIs to check if a functional dependency holds, *apriori-gen* to ensure that all minimal functional dependencies are found, and *pruning rules* to reduce the search space.

Similar to other lattice traversal algorithms, TANE models the search space as a Hasse diagram, as described in Section 4.2.1. Figure 4.5 depicts one such Hasse diagram for the relation $R = \{A, B, C\}$. The lattice consists of levels where each level $L_i$ contains all attribute combinations of size $i$. Instead of pre-calculating the entire lattice, TANE starts with Level 1 (attribute sets of size one) and then moves upward level by level (bold lines in the example). In level $L_i$, the algorithm tests all attribute combinations $X \in L_i$ for the functional dependency $X \setminus A \to A$ for all $A \in X$. The node $\{B, C\}$ in level 2, for instance, describes the FD candidates $B \to C$ and $C \to B$, which correspond to the two bold edges below that node. If a new functional dependency is found, TANE prunes all supersets of the discovered FD using a set of pruning rules. When moving upward to the next level, the *apriori-gen* function [Agrawal and Srikant, 1994] (see Section 4.3.2) generates only those attribute combinations from the previous level that have not been pruned.

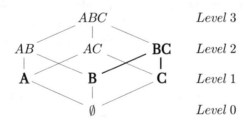

Figure 4.5: A pruned lattice used in TANE.

TANE's search space pruning is based on the fact that only *minimal* functional dependencies need to be discovered. To prune efficiently, the algorithm stores a set of right-hand side candidates $C^+(X)$ for each attribute combination $X$, defined as $C^+(X) = \{A \in R \mid \forall B \in X : X \setminus \{A, B\} \to B \ does \ not \ hold\}$. Each $C^+(X)$ contains only those attributes that may still form minimal FDs with $|X| - 1$ left-hand side attributes of $X$. The left-hand sides $X \setminus A$ can be minimal for only those $A \in C^+(X)$, where $X \setminus A$ has no inner FD, i.e., where there is no FD $X \setminus \{A, B\} \to B$ that would break the minimality of the left-hand side $X \setminus A$. During validation, the idea is to validate only those candidates $X \setminus A \to A$ where $A \in C^+(X)$. The set $C^+(X)$ is used in the following three pruning rules. We demonstrate an example run thereafter.

**Minimality pruning:** If $X \setminus A \to A$ holds, then $A$ and all $B \in C^+(X) \setminus X$ can be removed from $C^+(X)$. In other words, any FD $X \to B$ cannot be minimal if $X$ contains the FD $X \setminus A \to A$, because $A$ makes $X$ non-minimal. Note that this definition also includes $A = B$.

**Right-hand side pruning:** If $C^+(X) = \emptyset$, then the attribute combination $X$ can be pruned from the lattice because there are no more right-hand side candidates for a minimal functional dependency.

**Key pruning:** If the attribute combination $X$ is a key then it can be pruned because all supersets of $X$ are superkeys and are non-minimal by definition.

To check all possible FD candidates in a given lattice level, TANE uses *stripped partitions* a.k.a. PLIS $\hat{\pi}$, as described in Section 4.2.2. An FD $X \to A$ is valid iff $\widehat{\pi_X}$ refines $\widehat{\pi_{\{A\}}}$, i.e., each equivalence class in $\widehat{\pi_X}$ is contained within some equivalence class in $\widehat{\pi_{\{A\}}}$. While traversing the attribute lattice from bottom to top, TANE successively calculates the stripped partitions for new attribute combinations from their subsets via partition intersection.

A refinement check for an FD candidate is an expensive operation. Therefore, TANE optimizes these checks using the so-called *error measures*. The error measure $e(X)$ is the minimum fraction of tuples to remove from attribute combination $X$ to be a key. Each stripped partition holds such an error measure. It is calculated during the partition intersection operation that creates new stripped partitions. TANE checks the validity of an FD candidate $X \to A$ by testing if $e(X) = e(X \cup A)$. The special case $e(X) = 0$ means that $X$ is a key.

We now show an example run of TANE. Consider a relation $R = \{A, B, C, D\}$ and the (to be discovered) minimal FDs $C \to B$ and $AB \to D$. Through pseudo-transitivity $AC \to D$ is also valid. Table 4.4 shows the level sets $L_k$ and candidate sets $C^+$ for each level. Note that in Level 0, $L_0$ is empty. That is why we move directly to Level 1. In Level 1, each $C^+(X)$, which are $C^+(A)$, $C^+(B)$, $C^+(C)$, and $C^+(D)$, contains all attributes of the relation as RHS candidates of the empty set, all of them being false. In Level 2, we find $C \to B$ after checking all $A \to B$, $B \to A$, $A \to C$, etc., and prune the candidate set $C^+(BC)$ according to the first pruning rule. In Level 3, this also prunes the candidate set $C^+(ABC)$. Additionally, finding $AB \to D$ in Level 3 allows us to prune the candidates in $C^+(ABD)$. In Level 4, the candidate set $C^+(ABCD)$ is empty, which allows us to ignore the node according to the second pruning rule.

## 4.4.2  FUN

Similar to TANE, the FUN algorithm by Novelli and Cicchetti [2001] traverses the attribute lattice level-wise bottom-up and uses partition refinement to find functional dependencies. However, FUN explores a smaller portion of the search space through more restrictive candidate generation and a lazy look-up of *cardinality* values. The cardinality of an attribute combination $X$ is the number of its distinct value combinations. Like the error measure in TANE, this can be used to optimize the validation of FD candidates.

Table 4.4: An example run of TANE

| Level $L_k$ | Candidate Set $C^+$ |
|---|---|
| $L_0 = \emptyset$ | $C^+(\emptyset) = \{ABCD\}$ |
| $L_1 = \{A\}\{B\}\{C\}\{D\}$ | $C^+(A) = \{ABCD\}$, $C^+(B) = \{ABCD\}$ |
| | $C^+(C) = \{ABCD\}$, $C^+(D) = \{ABCD\}$ |
| | – nothing to check |
| $L_2 = \{AB\}\{AC\}\{AD\}$ $\{BC\}\{BD\}\{CD\}$ | $C^+(AB) = C^+(AB\backslash A) \cap C^+(AB\backslash B) = \{ABCD\}$, |
| | $C^+(AC) = C^+(AD) = C^+(BC) = C^+(BD) = C^+(CD) = \{ABCD\}$ |
| | – check $A{\to}B$, $B{\to}A$, $A{\to}C$, etc. |
| | – $C{\to}B$ is valid, so: |
| | delete $B$ and $R\backslash BC$ from $C^+(BC)$: $C^+(BC) = \{C\}$ |
| $L_3 = \{ABC\}\ \{ABD\}$ $\{ACD\}\ \{BCD\}$ | $C^+(ABC) = C^+(AB) \cap C^+(AC) \cap C^+(BC) = \{C\}$, |
| | $C^+(ABD) = C^+(ACD) = \{ABCD\}$, $C^+(BCD) = \{C\}$ |
| | – e.g., for $\{ABC\} \in L_3$ check only $ABC \cap C^+(ABC) = C$ as RHS, etc. |
| | – $AB{\to}D$ is valid, so: |
| | delete $D$ and $R\backslash ABD$ from $C^+(ABD)$: $C^+(ABD) = \{AB\}$ |
| | – $AC{\to}D$ is valid, so: |
| | delete $D$ and $R\backslash ACD$ from $C^+(ACD)$: $C^+(ACD) = \{AC\}$ |
| $L_4 = \{ABCD\}$ | $C^+(ABCD) = C^+(ABC) \cap C^+(ABD) \cap C^+(ACD) \cap C^+(BCD) = \emptyset$ |
| | – nothing left to check |

Instead of $C^+$ sets, FUN uses *free sets* and *non-free sets* to prune the search space. Free sets are sets of attributes that contain no element that is functionally dependent on any subset of the remaining elements. In other words, no FD exists among the attributes of a free set. The set of free sets $\mathcal{FS}$ is defined as follows.

**Definition 4.4** Let $X \subseteq R$ be a set of attributes in relation $R$, $r$ be a relational instance of $R$, and $|X|_r$ be the cardinality of the projection of $r$ over $X$, i.e., the number of distinct values in $X$. Then, $X \in \mathcal{FS}_r \Leftrightarrow \nexists X' \subset X : |X'|_r = |X|_r$.

Attribute sets that are not in $\mathcal{FS}_r$ are called non-free sets. Considering our previous example from the TANE algorithm (Section 4.4.1) with the three FDs $C \to B$, $AB \to D$, and $AC \to D$, we find that $\{A\}$, $\{A, D\}$, and $\{B, C, D\}$ are free sets because their attributes do not form any FD, and $\{C, B\}$, $\{A, B, D\}$, and $\{A, B, C, D\}$ are non-free sets because their attributes form FDs. Similar to TANE, FUN models the search space as a power set lattice of attribute combinations and starts traversing this lattice level-wise, bottom-up using *apriori-gen* candidate generation. The algorithm then classifies the nodes as either free or non-free sets, which naturally implements minimality pruning. Right-hand side and key pruning have also been adapted from TANE: only free sets that are non-unique column combinations, i.e., non-keys, are considered.

In some cases, the FUN algorithm is able to deduce the cardinality of attribute combinations from its subsets. This is possible if a set $X$ is known to be a non-free set. Then, one of the attributes of $X$ must be functionally dependent on one of the direct subsets of $X$. This implies that one of the direct subsets of $X$ has the same cardinality as $X$. This rule can be formalized as follows:

$$\forall X \notin \mathcal{FS}_r, \forall X' \subset X : X' \in \mathcal{FS}_r \Rightarrow |X|_r = Max(|X'|_r). \tag{4.1}$$

Deducing cardinality values allows FUN to prune attribute combinations more aggressively than TANE. All non-free sets can be pruned because if the cardinality of a superset is needed later, the algorithm can infer this cardinality from the superset's subsets. TANE, on the other hand, needs to process such candidate sets further until their $C^+$ sets become empty. Hence, cardinality deduction gives FUN a performance advantage over TANE. The following example, illustrated in Figure 4.6, explains this pruning and deduction process in more detail.

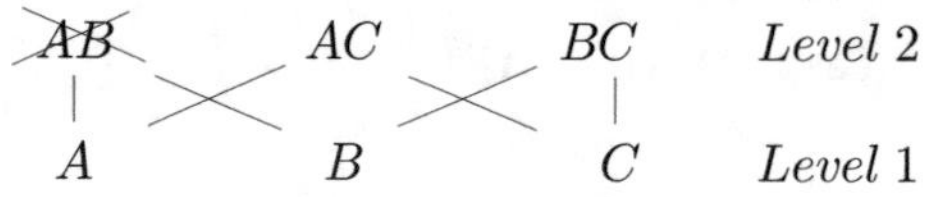

$$AB \qquad AC \qquad BC \qquad Level\ 2$$
$$A \qquad B \qquad C \qquad Level\ 1$$

Figure 4.6: Pruned example lattice for FUN.

Consider a schema $R = \{A, B, C\}$ and the minimal functional dependencies $A \to B$ and $BC \to A$. In level $L_1$, FUN checks all FD candidates with arity one (the lattice edges from level $L_1$ to $L_2$) and discovers $A \to B$. This prunes the lattice node $AB$ from level $L_2$ because we now know that it is a non-free set. Furthermore, the node $ABC$ is pruned from level $L_3$ because its subset $AB$ was pruned; hence, it is not a candidate for the left-hand side of any FD. To check and find $BC \to A$ in the next level $L_2$, FUN needs to compare the cardinality of $BC$ and $ABC$. As the node $ABC$ is pruned, it must be a non-free set and its cardinality can be deduced from its direct subsets using Equation 4.1, i.e., we check the cardinalities of $AB$, $AC$, and $BC$ and select their max cardinality for $ABC$.

The cardinality look-up is implemented by a method called *fastCount()*. According to Equation 4.1, this method calculates the cardinality of a non-free set as the maximum cardinality of its direct subsets. However, the direct subsets may have been pruned and therefore their cardinalities may not have been calculated. Therefore, cardinality look-up needs to be implemented recursively. To enable recursive look-up, FUN needs to keep the cardinality values of all previous levels in memory.

### 4.4.3   FD_MINE

The FD_MINE algorithm by Yao et al. [2002] is the third algorithm that—like TANE and FUN—traverses the attribute lattice level-wise bottom-up, and uses stripped partitions and partition intersections to discover functional dependencies. It also builds upon TANE's pruning rules. However, FD_MINE uses an additional pruning rule that is based on equivalence classes of attribute sets. Two attribute sets are considered *equivalent* with respect to their implied partition ($\Leftrightarrow_\pi$) iff they functionally depend on each other:

$$\forall X, Y \subseteq R : (X \Leftrightarrow_\pi Y) \Leftrightarrow X \rightarrow Y \wedge Y \rightarrow X. \tag{4.2}$$

Whenever a level in the attribute lattice has been validated, FD_MINE scans the discovered FDs and checks for equivalent FDs. If equivalent attribute sets are found, FD_MINE can prune all but one of each group from the lattice because their functional dependencies can be reconstructed according to the following properties:

$$\forall W, X, Y, Z \subseteq R : (X \Leftrightarrow_\pi Y) \wedge XW \rightarrow Z \Rightarrow YW \rightarrow Z \tag{4.3}$$

$$\forall W, X, Y, Z \subseteq R : (X \Leftrightarrow_\pi Y) \wedge WZ \rightarrow X \Rightarrow WZ \rightarrow Y. \tag{4.4}$$

Given Properties 4.3 and 4.4, the pruning rule guarantees that the derived functional dependencies hold, but it does not assert their minimality. Thus, the additional pruning rule implemented in FD_MINE helps to reduce the number of refinement checks, but it comes at the cost of minimality. To report only minimal FDs, FD_MINE would need to apply a post-processing step that is as complex as the discovery of FDs, as it corresponds to a top-down FD discovery algorithm. Moreover, the memory footprint of FD_MINE can be larger than that of TANE and FUN due to the need to maintain non-minimal intermediate results. Thus, the non-minimal FDs found by FD_MINE pose a performance issue that outweighs the performance gains of omitted refinement checks.

### 4.4.4   DFD

DFD by Abedjan et al. [2014c] is similar to its UCC discovery counterpart DUCC, which we introduced in Section 4.3.3. It models the search space as a lattice of attribute combinations and uses a depth-first random-walk traversal strategy. The difference is that candidate validation and pruning rules are designed for FDs instead of UCCs.

In TANE, the search space is a lattice of attribute combinations, and by subtracting individual attributes in each node, TANE checks all edges below that node for potential FDs. In contrast, the random walk of DFD models the search space as *multiple* lattices, each one modeling the possible left-hand sides for one specific right-hand side. In particular, DFD constructs $|R|$ lattices, one for each RHS attribute $A \in R$ holding the LHS attributes $R \setminus A$. FD candidates are represented as nodes, not edges. Similar to UCC discovery, valid *minimal* dependencies, which are the dependencies that DFD aims to discover, separate valid and invalid dependencies along a virtual border. Traversing this virtual border maximizes the effect of up- and downward pruning. When processing the lattices one after another, the random walk uses what the authors call *decidable paths*. This means that at any node in the lattice, DFD knows if the next node to visit should be smaller or larger.

Lattice traversal starts by choosing one node from a set of seed nodes, which are the nodes at the bottom of the lattice. DFD then classifies this node as a *dependency* or *non-dependency*, also checking for minimality/maximality properties. If the node is a dependency, DFD prunes its supersets using the same pruning rules as TANE and continues with a random, unvisited child node. If the node is a non-dependency, DFD prunes its subsets by classifying them as non-dependencies and continues with a random, unvisited parent node. When DFD cannot find an unvisited node in the appropriate direction, it backtracks to a previous node in the path or, if the entire path has been processed, to a new seed node to continue from there.

Due to superset and subset pruning, islands of unclassified candidate nodes can appear in the lattice. DFD finds these islands in a post-processing step by complementing the discovered maximum non-dependencies and checking them against the discovered minimal dependencies. All nodes in the complement set must be valid dependencies, i.e., they must be known minimal FDs or supersets of them; if they are not, they are unclassified candidate nodes and serve as new seeds.

Like all lattice-based algorithms, DFD uses partition refinement to validate dependency candidates. Once calculated, the stripped partitions, i.e., PLIs, are kept in memory for later use. In contrast to the previously described algorithms, DFD dynamically evicts stripped partitions when memory is exhausted. For this purpose, DFD calculates usage counts for the stripped partitions and removes less often used partitions when memory is needed. Some partitions, therefore, need to be calculated more than once.

### 4.4.5    DEP-MINER

The DEP-MINER algorithm by Lopes et al. [2000] infers all minimal functional dependencies from sets of attributes that have the same values in pairs of tuples. These sets are called *agree sets* and their inverse *difference sets*. DEP-MINER can be divided into five phases as shown in Figure 4.7. In Phase 1, DEP-MINER computes the stripped partition $\widehat{\pi_A}$ for each attribute. The $\widehat{\pi_A}$ are then used in Phase 2 to build all agree sets $ag(r)$. Phase 3 transforms agree sets into maximal sets, i.e., sets of attributes that have no superset with the same values in two records of $r$. In Phase 4, DEP-MINER inverts agree sets into complement sets. From the complement sets, the algorithm calculates all minimal FDs in Phase 5. For this purpose, it uses a level-wise search over the complement sets. Since the calculation of stripped partitions in Phase 1 is the same as in all other PLI-based algorithms, we describe only Phases 2–5 in more detail.

**Phase 2:** An agree set $ag(t_i, t_j)$ is defined pairwise between tuples $t_i$ and $t_j$ of $r$: $ag(t_i, t_j) = \{A \in R \mid t_i[A] = t_j[A]\}$ where $t_i[A]$ denotes the value of tuple $t_i$ in attribute A. To calculate all

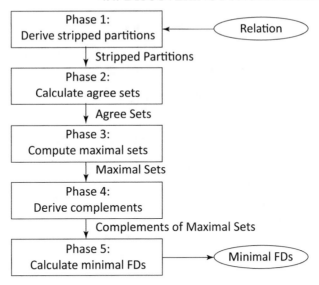

Figure 4.7: Phases of DEP-MINER.

agree sets of a given relational instance, DEP-MINER uses the so-called *identifier sets* $ec(t)$. The identifier set $ec(t)$ is defined as follows.

**Definition 4.5**　Let $R$ be a relational schema, $t$ a tuple identifier and $\widehat{\pi_{A,i}}$ the $i$th equivalence class of $\widehat{\pi_A}$. Then, $ec(t) := \{(A, i) \mid A \in R \wedge t \in \widehat{\pi_{A,i}}\}$.

In other words, $ec(t)$ describes the relationship between a tuple $t$ and all partitions containing $t$. Agree sets can now be calculated by intersecting identifier sets $ag(t_i, t_j) = ac(t_i) \cap ac(t_j)$. Consider the following example. Assume that $\widehat{\pi_A} = \{\widehat{\pi_{A,0}}, \widehat{\pi_{A,1}}\}$, and $\widehat{\pi_B} = \{\widehat{\pi_{B,0}}, \widehat{\pi_{B,1}}\}$ with $\widehat{\pi_{A,0}} = \{1, 2\}$, $\widehat{\pi_{A,1}} = \{3, 4\}$, $\widehat{\pi_{B,0}} = \{1, 4\}$, and $\widehat{\pi_{B,1}} = \{2, 3\}$. Then, the identifier set for tuple 1 is $ec(1) = \{(A, 0), (B, 0)\}$ and for tuple 2 it is $ec(2) = \{(A, 0), (B, 1)\}$. To obtain $ag(1, 2)$, we calculate the intersection of $ec(1)$ and $ec(2)$, which is $\{(A, 0)\}$. Removing the index, we find $ag(1, 2) = \{A\}$.

Since the same tuple can be contained in multiple stripped partitions (corresponding to different attributes), DEP-MINER may compare a pair of tuples $(t_i, t_j)$ multiple times. To reduce the number of redundant comparisons, $\hat{\pi}$ is first transformed into its maximal representation $MC = Max_{\subseteq}\{c \in \hat{\pi} \mid \hat{\pi} \in \hat{r}\}$, where $\hat{r}$ is the set of all stripped partitions of $r$.

The following example shows how $MC$ avoids redundant comparisons. Let $\hat{\pi}_A = \{\{1, 2\}\}$ and $\hat{\pi}_B = \{\{1, 2, 3\}\}$. Without computing the $MC$, the algorithm compares tuple pairs $(1, 2)$ for $\hat{\pi}_A$ and $(1, 2)$, $(1, 3)$, and $(2, 3)$ for $\hat{\pi}_B$. By computing $MC = \{\{1, 2, 3\}\}$, the tuple pair comparisons reduce to $(1, 2)$, $(1, 3)$, $(2, 3)$, i.e., $(1, 2)$ is compared only once.

**Phase 3:** From the agree sets, DEP-MINER calculates, for each attribute $A$, the maximal sets $max(dep(r), A)$, where $dep(r)$ denotes the set of all FDs in $r$. A maximal set contains all free sets that (i) do not include the attribute $A$ and (ii) have no subsets in the maximal set. Hence, all agree sets in $max(dep(r), A)$ nearly functionally determine $A$:

$$max(dep(r), A) := \{X \subseteq R \mid X \nrightarrow A \wedge \forall Y \subseteq R, X \subset Y, Y \rightarrow A\}.$$

Maximal sets can be computed from agree sets using the following equation:

$$max(dep(r), A) = Max_{\subseteq}\{X \in ag(r) \mid A \notin X, X \neq \emptyset\}. \tag{4.5}$$

**Phase 4:** Maximal sets describe maximal non-FDs. To derive minimal FDs, DEP-MINER computes the complement $cmax(dep(r), A)$ of the maximal sets $max(dep(r), A)$ for each $A \in R$. This can be done by calculating $R \backslash X$ for all $X \in max(dep(r), A)$.

**Phase 5:** In the last phase, DEP-MINER generates the left-hand sides of all minimal FDs with right-hand side $A$ from $cmax(dep(r), A)$ for each attribute $A \in R$. To do this, the algorithm searches level-wise through the complement sets in $cmax(dep(r), A)$. The first level is initialized with all unary attribute sets $\{B\} \in cmax(dep(r), A)$. Next, the algorithm moves upward level by level to infer minimal FDs. In level $L_i$, given some $X \in L_i$, the functional dependency $X \rightarrow A$ holds iff $\forall Y \in cmax(dep(r), A) : X \cap Y \neq \emptyset$. Before generating the next level, DEP-MINER removes all attribute sets $X$ from $L_i$ that yielded valid left-hand sides to ensure that only minimal functional dependencies are found. Then, the generation of level $L_{i+1}$ from level $L_i$ uses an adapted version of the *apriori-gen* algorithm. DEP-MINER terminates when the generation of the next level results in no further candidates for each $A \in R$.

### 4.4.6    FASTFDS

The FASTFDs algorithm by Wyss et al. [2001] builds on DEP-MINER and also uses agree sets to derive functional dependencies. After calculating agree sets in Phase 2, FASTFDs follows a different strategy to derive minimal functional dependencies. Since maximizing agree sets in Phase 3 of DEP-MINER is expensive, FASTFDs instead calculates all *difference sets* as $\mathcal{D}_r := \{R \backslash X \mid X \in ag(r)\}$ directly on the agree sets $ag(r)$. In Phase 4, the algorithm calculates the difference sets of $r$ modulo $A$ as $\mathcal{D}_r^A := \{D - \{A\} \mid D \in \mathcal{D}_r \wedge A \in D\}$. The $\mathcal{D}_r^A$ sets are FAST-FDs' equivalent to complement sets $cmax(dep(r), A)$ used in DEP-MINER and also enable the derivation of minimal functional dependencies. With the $\mathcal{D}_r^A$ sets, FASTFDs reduces the problem of finding all minimal FDs to the problem of finding all *minimal covers* over $\mathcal{D}_r^A$. A minimal cover is defined as follows.

**Definition 4.6**    Let $\mathcal{P}(R)$ be the power set of the relation $R$ and $\mathcal{X} \subseteq \mathcal{P}(R)$. The attribute set $X \subseteq R$ is called a *cover* for $\mathcal{X}$ iff $\forall Y \in \mathcal{X}, Y \cap X \neq \emptyset$. Furthermore, X is a *minimal cover* for $\mathcal{X}$ iff X covers $\mathcal{X}$ and $\nexists Z \subset X$ such that $Z$ is a cover for $\mathcal{X}$.

To retrieve FDs from minimal covers, FastFDs uses Lemma 4.4.1.

**Lemma 4.4.1** *Let $X \subseteq R$ and $A \notin X$. Then $X \rightarrow A$ iff $X$ covers $\mathcal{D}_r^A$.*

To find minimal covers for all $\mathcal{D}_r^A$, FastFDs constructs a search tree for each possible right-hand side $A \in R$. Figure 4.8 shows an example. Each node of the tree stores the difference sets that are not already covered and the current attribute ordering $>_{curr}$. The attribute ordering orders all attributes contained in $\mathcal{D}_r^A$ by the number of difference sets that they cover. Attributes that cover the same number of difference sets are ordered lexicographically.

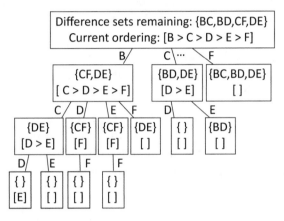

Figure 4.8: Example search tree for attribute $A$.

To calculate minimal covers, FastFDs traverses the tree depth-first. A greedy heuristic that always chooses the highest ordered attribute in $>_{curr}$ decides which attribute and therefore which branch of the tree should be investigated next. If the search visits a node for which $>_{curr} = \emptyset$ but it still holds uncovered difference sets, the set of chosen attributes $X$ within this branch is not a cover for $\mathcal{D}_r^A$ and, hence, $X \rightarrow A$ does not hold. On the other hand, if FastFDs reaches a node that contains no more difference sets to cover, the set of attributes $X$ within this branch is a cover for $\mathcal{D}_r^A$. Because of Lemma 4.4.1, the functional dependency $X \rightarrow A$ then holds. However, FastFDs still needs to ensure that this dependency is minimal by investigating its left hand side. The algorithm has discovered all minimal functional dependencies when the search tree has been traversed for each attribute $A \in R$.

FastFDs improves Dep-Miner by minimizing difference sets instead of maximizing agree sets. On some datasets (often those that contain many FDs), minimizing difference sets is much more efficient than maximizing agree sets. However, FastFDs is known to be less efficient than other FD discovery algorithms.

### 4.4.7   FDEP

The FDEP algorithm by Flach and Savnik [1999] is not based on candidate generation or attribute set analysis. Instead, the algorithm successively specializes a set of minimal FDs (or maximal non-FDs) by pairwise comparing all tuples. The authors propose three variants of FDEP: top-down (specializing minimal FDs), bi-directional (specializing both FDs and non-FDs), and bottom-up (specializing maximal non-FDs). The best performance is achieved by the bottom-up variant that successively specializes minimal FDs.

The bottom-up FDEP consists of two steps: negative cover construction and negative cover inversion. The *negative cover* is a set of all non-FDs that have been found when comparing all records pairwise. Consider, for example, a schema $R(A, B, C, D)$ with two tuples $t_1(1, 1, 2, 2)$ and $t_2(1, 3, 3, 3)$. From the comparison of $t_1$ and $t_2$ we fetch the non-FDs $A \nrightarrow B, C, D$, because $t_1$ and $t_2$ have the same value of $A$ but different values of $B$, $C$, and $D$. After calculating all non-FDs, i.e., the entire negative cover, its inverse, the *positive cover*, is exactly the set of all minimal FDs. Below, we first describe the *FD-tree* data structure that stores negative and positive covers. Then, we describe the two steps of FDEP.

**FD-Tree:** An *FD-tree* is an extended prefix tree that stores functional dependencies $X \rightarrow A$. Three example *FD-trees* are shown in Figure 4.9. The root node represents the empty set and each node in the tree represents an attribute. Every path in the tree describes a left-hand side $X$. All nodes of such a path are labeled with the dependent attribute $A$ (technically, each node holds a bitset of size $|R|$ that has a 1-bit for every RHS attribute $A$ that uses this node for an LHS path). The last node of each path, i.e., the node that holds the last attribute of a valid LHS path, holds an extra flag (darker blue marked 1-bit in Figure 4.9) indicating that the path $X$ ends for RHS attribute $A$, such that $X \rightarrow A$ is a valid FD. In this way, the *FD-tree* efficiently represents FDs and non-FDs. A useful property of this data structure is that an algorithm can easily look up specializations (larger $X$) and generalizations (shorter $X$) of arbitrary FDs $X \rightarrow A$ via depth-first search.

**Negative cover construction:** FDEP first builds a negative cover, which contains all dependencies that cannot hold. The negative cover is initialized to an empty *FD-tree*. Then, FDEP compares all pairs of tuples $t_i, t_j \in r$. Each comparison extracts attribute sets $X$ that have equal values in $t_i$ and $t_j$. It follows that all dependencies $X \rightarrow A$ with $A \in R \setminus X$ cannot be valid in $r$, which means that $X \rightarrow R \setminus X$ is a non-FD. Once identified, FDEP adds all such non-FDs to the negative cover.

After comparing all pairs of records, the negative cover contains all invalid FDs. Since most of the non-FDs in the cover are not maximal, FDEP filters all generalizations out of the *FD-tree* in a post-processing step. However, because the next step of the algorithm does not require the negative cover to be maximal, a more efficient way of preparing the negative cover for the next step is to simply sort all contained non-FDs in descending order by their LHS size, as shown in Papenbrock and Naumann [2016].

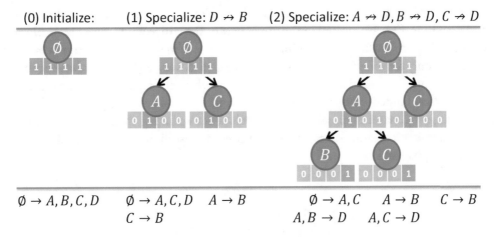

Figure 4.9: Specializing the FDTree with non-FDs.

**Negative cover inversion:** The second step calculates a positive cover from the negative cover via successive specialization. Figure 4.9 shows this specialization process from left to right in three steps for four non-FDs. First, FDEP initializes a new *FD-tree* with the most general FDs $\emptyset \to A$ for all $A \in R$ (see the first tree in Figure 4.9). Then, the algorithm incrementally specializes this *FD-tree* with non-FDs from the negative cover. For each non-FD $X \to A$ in the negative cover, FDEP recursively collects all its generalizations (and the non-FD itself if present) from the positive cover because these must be invalid as well. In our example, the only invalid specialization of $D \not\to B$ in the positive cover is $\emptyset \to B$. FDEP then successively removes the retrieved non-FDs from the positive cover. Once removed, a non-FD is specialized, which means that the algorithm *extends* the LHS of the non-FD with every possible (i.e., not already contained) attribute to generate valid specializations. In our example, these are $A \to B$ and $C \to B$. Before adding these specializations back to the positive cover, the Inductor ensures that the new FDs are minimal by searching for generalizations among the known FDs. Figure 4.9 also shows the result when inducing three more non-FDs into the *FD-tree*. After specializing the positive cover with all FDs in the negative cover, the prefix-tree holds the entire set of valid, minimal FDs.

### 4.4.8   HYFD

HYFD by Papenbrock and Naumann [2016] is a hybrid discovery algorithm for functional dependencies that combines column-efficient search properties of dependency induction algorithms—FDEP in this case—with row-efficient search properties of lattice traversal algorithms—a TANE-based strategy. HYFD is similar to the unique column combination discovery algorithm HYUCC as it also switches back and forth between the two strategies, depending on which strategy performs best at the time.

We first revisit the search space lattice for FDs. Figure 4.10 shows an example lattice with FDs and non-FDs. FDs are located in the upper part of the lattice while non-FDs are located at the bottom. We distinguish between minimal and non-minimal FDs because a discovery algorithm searches only for minimal FDs. Similar to UCC discovery, a virtual border separates valid dependencies from the invalid ones. All minimal FDs, which the algorithm aims to discover, reside on this virtual border. HYFD uses this observation as follows: via sampling and dependency induction, it approximates minimal FDs from below, thus pruning many low-level candidates; via PLI-based validations and lattice traversal, it prunes most high-level non-minimal FDs and produces a complete and exact result.

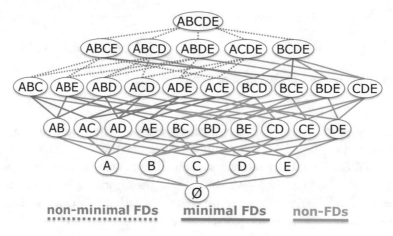

Figure 4.10: A lattice for FD discovery.

**Dependency induction phase:** The first phase of HYFD uses FDEP, i.e., it compares records pairwise, derives non-FDs, and turns these non-FDs into valid, minimal FDs. However, HYFD avoids comparing all record pairs and instead compares only a small sample of them. The algorithm then stores the negative cover, i.e., the discovered non-FDs, in a set of bitsets because this data structure is in practice much smaller than an *FD-tree*. The two tuples $t_1(2, Eve, Smith, 24, 5432)$ and $t_2(3, Eve, Payne, 24, 3333)$ of schema Person(id, first, last, age, phone), for example, yield the bitset $b_{1,2}[0, 1, 0, 1, 0]$ as $t_1$ and $t_2$ match only in the values "*Eve*" (index 1) and 24 (index 3). Therefore, {first, age} $\not\to$ id, last, phone are three non-FDs encoded by $b_{1,2}$. Because sorting the bitsets by their cardinality (= number of 1-bits) in descending order before inducing the positive cover has the same effect but lower cost than maximizing the negative cover as done by FDEP, this data structure is also more efficient than an *FD-tree* for storing the non-FDs.

Since the induced FD candidates are based on a sample of record pairs, the algorithm may have missed some violating record pairs. Thus, the candidates must be validated. Nevertheless, the candidates have three useful properties. First, they are *complete* in the sense that they contain or imply all true FDs. Second, they are *minimal* or imply minimal FDs. Third, they are closer to true FDs (in terms of the number of attributes) than candidates at the bottom of the lattice, which provides pruning opportunities because many FD candidates are directly inferred to be non-FDs without explicit validation. In summary, the idea of the dependency induction phase is to produce a superset of minimal FD candidates that are close to the true minimal FDs.

When choosing record pairs to examine, HyFD considers only those records that co-occur in at least one PLI cluster—all other record pairs have no value in common and therefore cannot violate any FD. The algorithm prioritizes record pairs that share many PLI clusters because such record pairs violate FDs in higher lattice levels and therefore prune many candidates at once. To find these record pairs, HyFD proposes a *focused sampling* method. The algorithm first sorts the records in all PLI clusters by their cluster number in *other* PLIs, bringing together records that share the same clusters. Then, it runs a small window over these clusters, comparing all records within this window. Windows that revealed the most FD violations are enlarged and re-run until they become *inefficient*, meaning that the ratio of newly discovered FD violations per pairwise comparison has fallen below a pre-defined threshold, e.g., less than one new violation in one hundred comparisons. In that case, HyFD switches to the lattice traversal phase.

**Lattice traversal phase:** The second phase of HyFD uses the row-efficient bottom-up breadth-first lattice traversal strategy of TANE. However, instead of validating each candidate in the lattice, HyFD directly operates on the candidates provided by the dependency induction phase. Many of these candidates are true FDs or have already been falsified. HyFD also executes all validations of the same lattice level in parallel—an optimization that would also work for TANE, FUN, and FD_MINE because these validations are independent from one another.

The third difference between HyFD and other lattice traversal algorithms is that HyFD does not cache intermediate PLIs. Like the UCC discovery algorithm HyUCC, HyFD validates FDs using single-column PLIs. The idea is to calculate the intersections of LHS PLIs dynamically while at the same time checking if the resulting LHS PLI clusters refine the RHS PLI. Figure 4.11 illustrates this approach with an example. The algorithm first iterates over all the clusters of the first LHS PLI, which is the PLI of attribute $X_0$, where $X_0 \in X$. For each record $r_i$ in a cluster, the algorithm looks up this record's clusters in all other LHS PLIs. In this way, it retrieves a set of LHS cluster identifiers, i.e., a cluster tuple that serves as a cluster identifier for the entire LHS of a particular record. The validation algorithm then maps this cluster tuple to the record's RHS cluster identifier, which can be retrieved from the RHS PLI. If the map already contains a mapping for the current LHS cluster tuple, then the RHS cluster also needs to be the same and the algorithm can ignore the new mapping. Otherwise, if the RHS cluster identifiers differ, the algorithm has found a violation, i.e., the current intersection step produced a refinement violation, and it can stop the validation process. The last record and the record whose entry was already placed into the map constitute the violation. In our example, $r_5$ and $r_8$ share the LHS cluster identifier $(0, 1, 0)$, which maps to the same RHS cluster identifier 4, indicating no violation. Furthermore, $r_3$ and $r_6$ violate the FD $X \to Y_i$ because they share the LHS cluster identifier $(2, 1, 4)$ and differ in their RHS cluster identifiers, which are 0 and 3.

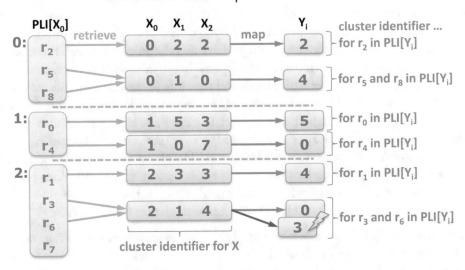

Figure 4.11: Validation of the FD $X \to Y_i$ via dynamic PLI intersection. Note that $X_i$ denotes the $i$th attribute in the LHS attribute set $X$, so $X_i \in X$. The map **PLI** stores, for every attribute $A$ (in particular for $X_0$), its single column PLI $\phi_A$. The cluster identifiers for both $X$ and $Y_i$ are read from the inverted index.

Lattice traversal stops if the search becomes inefficient. In this phase, inefficiency means that the ratio of true FDs per non-FD falls below a threshold. Whenever this happens, HYFD switches back into the dependency induction phase. If all candidates have been classified as true FDs or non-FDs, the algorithm terminates and outputs the discovered minimal FDs.

**Hybrid search:** When switching back and forth between the two phases, HYFD ensures that both phases support each other. The induction phase sends a pre-pruned search space to the traversal phase and the traversal phase sends record pairs that caused a violation as suggestions to the induction phase. HYFD also dynamically reduces the efficiency threshold of the induction phase so that the sampling process can run more windows and therefore compare more tuple pairs. On the other hand, the threshold of the traversal phase is not adjusted because validation efficiency should not decrease.

The performance of various functional dependency discovery algorithms has been experimentally tested in Papenbrock et al. [2015b] and Papenbrock and Naumann [2016] on various datasets. As expected, lattice traversal algorithms perform best on datasets with many rows while dependency induction algorithms perform best on datasets with many columns. The hybrid algorithm scales well in both dimensions—it even outperforms the best individual strategy on each dataset due to the synergy effects of hybrid search.

Although the datasets in their experiments were small (5 KB to 69 MB), they already show the limits of row- and column-based strategies. However, the hybrid algorithm can process larger datasets; as shown in Papenbrock and Naumann [2016], it processed tables with sizes around 1–8 GB in 4 min to 8 h. These datasets cover real-world biological, enterprise, and address data. Thus, when used together, state-of-the-art FD discovery techniques can process datasets of typical real-world sizes in reasonable time. However, datasets of many dozens of gigabytes or even terabytes are most likely too large for today's FD profiling algorithms.

## 4.5   DISCOVERING INCLUSION DEPENDENCIES

As discussed in Section 4.2, discovering INDs is different from discovering other types of dependencies. First, the search space is larger because INDs are defined across multiple tables. Second, IND pruning rules work in the opposite direction to FD pruning rules: *supersets* of non-INDs are also non-INDs and *subsets* of true INDs are also true INDs because true dependencies lie at the bottom of the lattice and not at the top. Third, PLI indexes (stripped partitions) cannot be used because INDs need to examine actual values (not just to verify if two values are equal). Finally, most IND discovery algorithms use different null semantics.

Due to these differences, IND-specific techniques have been proposed. For instance, lattice traversal strategies follow not only classical bottom-up, random-walk, and top-down procedures, but also bi-directional, clique-based, and coordinate-based approaches. Since the input is large (many tables) and not compressed (no PLIs), utilizing the disk as secondary storage is crucial during IND discovery. Inclusion dependency checks map to join operations, so many discovery algorithms perform these checks through the underlying database management system (via SQL).

Table 4.5 lists the popular algorithms for exact IND discovery with the arity of INDs that they discover, their validation and traversal strategy, and a description of key ideas. The table shows that the algorithms specialize in different arities of INDs, i.e., some discover only unary INDs while others require unary INDs as input and discover only n-ary INDs. Depending on the arity, their main contribution is either an efficient strategy to validate IND candidates (unary algorithms) or an efficient strategy to minimize the number of candidate validations while traversing the search space (n-ary algorithms).

Since all current discovery algorithms are lattice-based to some extent, we propose a different classification that separates them by their main contribution as *candidate validation algorithms* or *lattice traversal algorithms*.

**Candidate validation algorithms:** One task in IND discovery is to efficiently validate a set of IND candidates. Validating a single candidate is essentially a join and candidate validation algorithms aim to execute these joins as efficiently as possible. They propose different strategies

Table 4.5: Popular algorithms for exact IND discovery listed with the arity of INDs that they discover, their validation and traversal strategy, and a description of their key ideas

| Algorithm | INDs | Validation | Traversal | Ideas |
|---|---|---|---|---|
| B&B | unary | SQL | - | statistical and axiomatic pruning |
| DeMarchi | unary | algorithmic | - | hash-join; in-memory |
| Binder | both | algorithmic | bottom-up | hash-join; stopping; disk-backed |
| Spider | unary | algorithmic | - | sort-merge-join; stopping; disk-backed |
| S-IndD | unary | algorithmic | - | sort-merge-join; stopping; disk-backed |
| Sindy | unary | algorithmic | - | hash-join; massively parallel |
| Mind | n-ary | SQL | bottom-up | apriori-based candidate generation |
| Find2 | n-ary | SQL | clique-based | candidates from hypergraph-cliques |
| ZigZag | n-ary | SQL | bi-directional | optimistic and pessimistic borders |
| Mind2 | n-ary | algorithmic | coordinate-based | iterative merging of IND coordinates |

that, for instance, check candidates simultaneously to avoid redundant operations, terminate joins as soon as a violation has been found to prune superfluous value checks, spill data to disk to control memory consumption, and utilize massive parallelization. Algorithms in this category are B&B [Bell and Brockhausen, 1995], DeMarchi [Marchi et al., 2009], Binder [Papenbrock et al., 2015d], Spider [Bauckmann et al., 2006], S-IndD [Shaabani and Meinel, 2015], and Sindy [Kruse et al., 2015a].

**Lattice traversal algorithms:** When discovering n-ary INDs, the number of candidates grows exponentially with every lattice level. Checking all candidates is usually infeasible regardless of the validation technique being used. Lattice traversal algorithms, therefore, use axiomatic rules to prune the search space. While the axioms are the same for all traversal algorithms, the effectiveness of pruning differs depending on where the true INDs lie in the lattice. Algorithms in the lattice traversal category are Mind [Marchi et al., 2009], Find2 [Koeller and Rundensteiner, 2003], ZigZag [Marchi and Petit, 2003], and Mind2 [Shaabani and Meinel, 2016]. While Mind assumes most INDs are in lower lattice levels, which can best be reached with a bottom-up search, Find2, ZigZag, and Mind2 assume most INDs reside on higher lattice levels, which require more aggressive traversal strategies. Depending on where the n-ary INDs actually are, one strategy or another performs best. All lattice traversal algorithms assume that unary INDs are given, i.e., they assume that some unary discovery algorithm has already discovered them.

**Null Semantics:** For INDs, null semantics do not specify whether null $\neq$ null or null = null because we treat all null values as *no value*. This means that IND checks can ignore null values, i.e., a null value in an Lhs attribute does not require a matching null value in an

Rʜs attribute. This interpretation aligns with the meaning of referential integrity constraints in relational databases, where every value in a dependent column must either be a value from the referenced column or `null`.

Another way of thinking about Lʜs `null` values is that they may hold any value from the Rʜs, i.e., we always find some *possible world* in which the IND is satisfied. However, a `null` value in the Rʜs does not match any Lʜs value. This is inconsistent (Lʜs `null`s match any Rʜs value; Rʜs `null`s match no Lʜs value), but is used in many discovery algorithms because `null` values may be assigned only once to create a consistent possible world and finding a consistent one-to-one substitution for all Rʜs `null`s is computationally complex.

N-ary INDs involve tuples that consist of multiple attributes that can be only partially `null`. For these values, we can also apply the *possible world* semantics: if the non-`null` part of the Lʜs value is included in the Rʜs values, the `null` part can take any co-occurring value. For example, if $(null, 1, 2)$ is an Lʜs value, $(\_, 1, 2)$ must be contained in the Rʜs values and `null` is considered as whatever value the wildcard operator _ matches on the Rʜs (here, an Lʜs `null` may match an Rʜs `null`, meaning `null = null`). Rʜs values with `null`s match Lʜs values with the same number of (or more) `null`s, but they do not match Lʜs values with other or fewer `null`s, e.g., the Rʜs value $(null, 1, 2)$ matches $(null, 1, 2)$, and $(null, null, 2)$, but not $(0, 1, 2)$ or $(0, null, 2)$.

Given the above `null` treatment, we now describe the algorithms in more detail. First, we discuss SQL-based candidate validation because many algorithms use this strategy (and we cannot clearly point out the algorithm that first proposed it). We then discuss IND discovery algorithms, starting with unary algorithms.

## 4.5.1 SQL-BASED IND VALIDATION

Many IND discovery algorithms are based on SQL queries that, given an IND candidate, test if all Lʜs values are contained in the Rʜs values. For efficiency, these SQL statements do not query all Lʜs values that find a match on the Rʜs; instead, they query those values that do *not* find a match. Thus, a query can terminate as soon as it finds the first Lʜs value that is not included in the candidate's Rʜs. One way to formulate this approach in a declarative SQL query is by specifying `limit 1` or `fetch first 1 rows only` (depending on the SQL dialect).

To check for missing Rʜs values, all SQL-based IND discovery algorithms we discuss use one of three popular options: an *outer join*, a *set operation*, or a *correlated subquery*. All three options have strengths and weaknesses and they may produce same or different execution plans depending on the query optimizer and DBMS. As an example, consider the IND candidate $R[A, B] \subseteq S[C, D]$ and the three validation queries shown in Figure 4.12. Here, we search for the first $A, B$-value that is not included in the set of $C, D$-values. If no such value exists, $R[A, B] \subseteq S[C, D]$ is valid.

All three queries ignore $A, B$-tuples with at least one `null` value although we do need to check the non-`null` part of these values. IND discovery algorithms query such special cases

| Outer Join | Set Operation | Correlated Subquery |
|---|---|---|

```
Outer Join                     Set Operation                  Correlated Subquery
SELECT A, B                    SELECT A, B                    SELECT A, B
FROM R LEFT OUTER JOIN S       FROM R                         FROM R
    ON A = C AND B = D         WHERE (A, B) NOT IN (          WHERE NOT EXISTS (
WHERE C IS NULL                    SELECT C, D                    SELECT *
AND    D IS NULL               FROM S                             FROM S
AND    A IS NOT NULL           )                                  WHERE A = C
AND    B IS NOT NULL           AND A IS NOT NULL                  AND B = D
LIMIT 1;                       AND B IS NOT NULL              )
                               LIMIT 1;                       AND A IS NOT NULL
                                                              AND B IS NOT NULL
                                                              LIMIT 1;
```

Figure 4.12: Three types of SQL validation queries: an *outer join* (left outer join), a *set operation* (not in), and a *correlated subquery* (not exists).

separately or—which is usually the case—infer these special cases from other INDs that they have already tested (see, for instance, the bottom-up lattice traversal in the MIND algorithm).

In the remainder of this section, we discuss each of the three SQL validation queries in more detail.

**Outer Join:** The *left outer join* calculates the join between the IND's LHS and RHS in order to list all LHS tuples with their RHS partner tuples. If there is no such partner tuple, the LHS is listed with null values. In such cases, i.e., when the LHS is not null but the entire RHS is null, the query found an IND-violating tuple because that particular LHS value is not included in the RHS.

In most database management systems, *left outer joins* provide the fastest SQL-based validation option because joins are highly optimized, may use indexes, and can use nested-loop-, hash-, or sort-based join procedures depending on which strategy performs best for a given IND candidate. Query optimizers will in general select an efficient join variant for each candidate. However, it is impossible for query optimizers to predict whether a join terminates early, i.e., whether the candidate is actually no IND. Therefore, join variants might also be chosen in a non-optimal way.

**Set Operation:** The *not in* IND validation query in Figure 4.12 tests every LHS value against the set of RHS values. If one such value is not included (and it does not contain null), it is an IND violation and the query can stop. The performance of the *not in* join depends very much on the query optimizer. Similar to the explicit *left outer join*, the *not in* join can, in general, use different join procedures, such as nested-loop-, hash-, or sort-based, and it can use indexes, if available. Also, the limit 1 clause enables early termination if one violation was found. The *not in* validation query can outperform *left outer joins* if the *left outer join* is badly optimized, e.g., if the join result is fully materialized before applying the `null` filters or if the join attributes are not projected before executing the join. On the other hand, *left outer joins* can outperform *not in* queries if they are executed as nested-loop-joins on large datasets with no violation that triggers early termination. In the best case, both strategies are optimized into same query execution plans for IND validations.

A problem with *not in* queries in the context of IND validation is that *not in* has different `null` semantics than the other two join options. It tests whether a given value is *different* from all values in the subquery. Thus, if the Rʜs contains one tuple that is entirely `null`, then the test against this value always yields `unknown`, which is effectively `false` for all Lʜs values. Hence, no value is selected, and, because we are looking for IND violations, all INDs with this Rʜs are assumed to be valid. From the semantic point of view, the Rʜs `null` value could be any Lʜs value and does, therefore, eliminate any IND violation. In practice, however, there can only be one substitution for the `null` value, so most checks with *not in* might be wrong.

The set operation *except*, which is the same as *minus*, does not have this problem. It also often translates into a physical query plan different from *not in*. An *except* query usually performs a full scan of both Lʜs and Rʜs attributes and then calculates the values that occur only in the Lʜs. For this reason, it is usually more efficient for validating true IND candidates rather than false ones.

In summary, modern database systems optimize both *not in* and *except* like *outer joins* and the underlying strategies use the same join variants. In the end, the query optimizer *might* turn all three validation queries into same physical query plans (especially in the absence of `null` values).

**Correlated Subquery:** The *not exists* operator creates a correlated subquery that checks whether each Lʜs value is absent from the Rʜs. There are three important differences between *not exists* and *not in*. First, *not exists* handles `null` values in the same way as *outer join* and *except*, and unlike *not in*, i.e., a `null` tuple on the Rʜs does not eliminate all potentially missing Lʜs values. This is because the comparison with `null` values is done *inside* the subquery; *not exists* checks many different subqueries while *not in* checks different values against the same subquery. This difference makes the *not exists* approach much slower than other solutions.

In general, correlated subqueries are more expressive than joins and set operations as they define more complicated interdependencies. As a result, it is harder for a query optimizer to automatically find efficient physical query plans—some structures might not even be recognized as joins and default to nested-loop plans.

Note that none of the SQL validation strategies works if the corresponding Lʜs and Rʜs attributes of the IND candidate do not have the same data types. Thus, SQL-based profiling algorithms will not find that, for instance, *numeric* elementary school grades are included in *floating point* high school grades or that *date*-formatted public holidays may refer to *string*-formatted calendar entries.

Furthermore, SQL queries require an underlying SQL execution engine, but some datasets may be stored as CSV, TSV, JSON, or XML files. Thus, we will also discuss alternative validation techniques for IND candidates in this section.

## 4.5.2   B&B

Bell and Brockhausen introduced the first algorithm that proposes a systematic discovery strategy to find *all* unary INDs for given relational instance [Bell and Brockhausen, 1995]. Since the authors did not name their algorithm, it is often referred to as the *Bell-and-Brockhausen* algorithm, or B&B. The algorithm validates IND candidates via SQL and, because these SQL checks are expensive, it prunes candidates using statistical and axiomatic pruning rules.

B&B collects statistics about all columns $X$, namely data types and min- and max-values. From all possible unary IND candidates $X \times X$, the algorithm selects attribute combinations $(A_i, A_j) \in X \times X$ as unary IND candidates $A_i \subseteq A_j$, where (1) $i \neq j$, (2) $type(A_i) = type(A_j)$, (3) $min(A_i) \geq min(A_j)$, (4) $max(A_i) \leq max(A_j)$, and (5) $count\_distinct(A_i) \leq count\_distinct(A_j)$. In other words, a unary IND candidate must be non-trivial, its Lhs and Rhs data types must match, the Lhs value range must lie within the Rhs value range, and the number of distinct values in the Lhs must be smaller than the number of distinct values in the Rhs. Checking these statistics prior to candidate validation may prune many candidates. However, this approach needs to check all possible $X \times X$ combinations for being viable IND candidates, so it has quadratic complexity.

Once IND candidates have been generated, B&B sorts them in ascending order by the Lhs attributes (primary sort) and the Rhs attributes (secondary sort). It then iterates over this list of candidates and validates them sequentially. For validation, the algorithm uses SQL-join statements as discussed in Section 4.5.1. Every true IND $A_i \subseteq A_j$ is inserted as an edge $(A_i, A_j)$ into a graph of attributes and triggers the following pruning rules.

**Positive rule:** If both $A_i \subseteq A_h$ and $A_h \subseteq A_j$ are true, then $A_i \subseteq A_j$ must be true by transitivity. If the new edge is $(A_i, A_h)$, i.e., from $A_i$ to $A_h$, and we already have the edge $(A_h, A_j)$, then the edge $(A_i, A_j)$ must exist. Thus, B&B inserts this transitive edge into the graph and does not have to validate the candidate $A_i \subseteq A_j$.

**Negative rule:** If $A_i \subseteq A_h$ is true and $A_h \subseteq A_j$ is false, then $A_i \subseteq A_j$ must be false by transitivity. If the new edge is $(A_i, A_h)$, but there is no edge $(A_h, A_j)$, then the edge $(A_i, A_j)$ cannot exist and the candidate $A_i \subseteq A_j$ does not have to be validated. This rule applies only to attribute indexes with $h < i$ because any edge $(A_h, A_j)$ is tested prior to the edge $(A_i, A_h)$ due to the sorting of IND candidates.

Although statistical and axiomatic pruning can reduce the candidate space, the B&B algorithm is by far the slowest algorithm in our list. However, a major advantage of B&B over most other IND discovery algorithms is that its memory footprint is very small because it pushes validation into the database layer and stores only the candidates and a few statistics in memory.

### 4.5.3   DEMARCHI

De Marchi et al. proposed an in-memory unary IND discovery algorithm, which is referred to as the DeMarchi algorithm [Marchi et al., 2009]. This algorithm builds an inverted index over the input dataset and performs an in-memory hash join of the dataset and the index to find valid INDs.

To construct the inverted index, DeMarchi reads the input once and maps every value to the attributes it occurs in. Figure 4.13 shows an example dataset with two relations and their inverted index. For example, the first value in the index, $a$, occurs in the attributes $A, C$, and $F$.

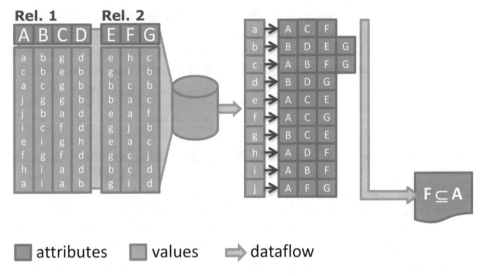

Figure 4.13: Visualization of DeMarchi's in-memory all-column hash join.

Each row (set of attributes) in the inverted index suggests that these attributes might be included in one another and cannot be included in other attributes. For instance, the attribute set $\{A, C, F\}$, corresponding to value $a$, indicates that $A \subseteq C$ and $A \subseteq F$ are possible INDs but $A \subseteq B, A \subseteq D, A \subseteq E$, and $A \subseteq G$ are all invalid because $B, D, E$, and $G$ do not have the value $a$.

The DeMarchi algorithm generates, for each attribute $A_i$, all possible IND candidates $A_i \subseteq X \setminus A_i$, where $X$ is the set of all attributes of all the input relations, $A_i$ is an Lhs attribute and $X \setminus A_i$ is the set of possible Rhs attributes for $A_i$. The candidates for attribute $A$ in our example are $A \subseteq \{B, C, D, E, F, G\}$, denoting the unary INDs $A \subseteq B, A \subseteq C, A \subseteq D$ and so on. At this point, it is easy to incorporate data type pruning by ignoring candidates whose Lhs and Rhs data types do not match.

To validate the candidates, the DeMarchi algorithm iterates over all attribute sets $S$ in the inverted index. For each $S$, it collects all IND candidates with Lhs attribute $A_i \in S$ from the candidate set and intersect their Rhs attribute set with $S$. Every intersect operation checks (and possibly removes) many IND candidates at once. The first intersect operation in our example uses the attribute set $\{A, C, F\}$ from the inverted index to collect the candidates $A \subseteq \{B, C, D, E, F, G\}$, $C \subseteq \{A, B, D, E, F, G\}$, and $F \subseteq \{A, B, C, D, E, G\}$. Then, it prunes these candidates to $A \subseteq \{C, F\}$, $C \subseteq \{A, F\}$, and $F \subseteq \{C, A\}$. All INDs with LHS attributes other than $A$, $C$, and $F$ remain unchanged. So for LHS attribute $A$, this one set operation removed four candidates, namely $A \subseteq B$, $A \subseteq D$, $A \subseteq E$, and $A \subseteq G$, and at the same time confirmed two other candidates, namely $A \subseteq C$ and $A \subseteq F$, with respect to value "a."

Intersect operations perform better than individual candidate validations via, for instance, SQL queries, as they check many candidates simultaneously. This strategy performs even better than statistical pruning introduced by the B&B algorithm. At some point, however, intersections repeat, i.e., the algorithm performs redundant intersections that do not rule out any further candidates. This is where the DEMARCHI algorithm falls short when compared to other validation approaches. It also requires the entire inverted index to fit into main memory, which is not always feasible.

### 4.5.4  BINDER

The algorithm BINDER, which is short for <u>B</u>ucketing <u>IN</u>clusion <u>D</u>ependency <u>E</u>xtracto<u>R</u>, is a memory-sensitive approach for the discovery of unary and n-ary INDs [Papenbrock et al., 2015d]. This means that the algorithm tries to fit as much data into main memory as possible, resorting to disk if main memory is exhausted. The algorithm also introduces several optimizations of the all-column hash-join validation process used in DEMARCHI: it uses a divide & conquer strategy to partition the input into smaller buckets that fit in main memory; it then checks these buckets for INDs with a special hash-join that adds a second index to DEMARCHI's validation procedure; and, using the apriori-gen algorithm for candidate generation, BINDER can also discover n-ary INDs.

Figure 4.14 depicts the validation process on two example relations. In the *divide phase*, BINDER reads all input relations once and splits the values in each column via hash-partitioning into a fixed number of buckets. A bucket receives all values with a certain hash for one attribute, which means that all values with the same hash are placed into the same bucket. With a good hash function, all buckets fill up evenly. Duplicate values are removed, and, if memory is exhausted during the bucketing process, BINDER spills the largest buckets to disk. In the end, all buckets are written to disk.

In the *conquer phase*, BINDER reads the buckets level-by-level back into main memory for candidate validation. One level of buckets contains all buckets that share the same hash, which is one bucket per attribute or, visually speaking, one row of boxes in Figure 4.14. If one level does not fit in memory, this level is re-bucketized exactly in the same way as the entire dataset was bucketized in the divide phase. The only difference is that the algorithm now knows the size of the level so that it can calculate the number of buckets needed to fit each sub-level of this level into main memory. Once a level has been loaded, BINDER constructs an inverted index

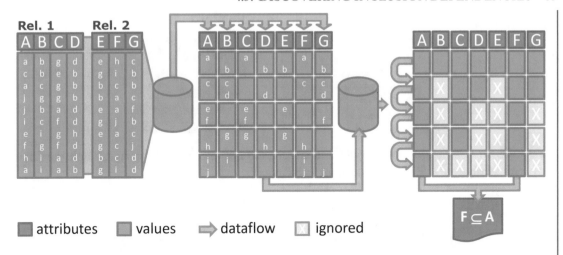

Figure 4.14: The divide and conquer phases of the BINDER algorithm by example.

(and an additional index) for this level and tests its IND candidates. Examining one level at a time avoids memory overflow and allows the algorithm to prune buckets of attributes whose IND candidates have all been falsified—if an attribute does not occur in any candidate, it is no longer needed for validation. As a result, the levels become smaller.

To validate IND candidates against one level of buckets, i.e., all values with the same hash, BINDER creates two indexes from these values: a dense index (*attr2value*) and an inverted index (*value2attr*). An example of these two indexes is shown in Figure 4.15. Given both indexes, BINDER iterates over all entries in *attr2value*. For each entry, it looks up each value in the *value2attr* list. If this entry still exists, BINDER takes the associated attribute set and performs the intersections with the corresponding IND candidate lists. Two aspects of this validation process avoid redundant intersection. First, whenever an entry in *value2attr* or *attr2value* has been handled, it is removed from the respective index to not be used again for candidate intersections. Second, BINDER stops processing entries in *value2attr* if the current key attribute in *attr2value* is not included in any other attribute, i.e., it is not an LHS attribute for any RHS.

Table 4.6 shows the validation process using the example indexes shown in Figure 4.15. Each column in the table represents a dependent LHS attribute and the cells list the RHS attributes that are referenced by the respective dependent attribute in each step. When reading the table row-wise from top to bottom, the initial IND candidates assume that each attribute is included in all three other attributes. The look-up process then starts with attribute $A$ in the *attr2values* index, reads its first value $a$ in *values2attr* and intersects $a$'s attribute set $\{A, C\}$ with the RHS attributes of $A$ and $C$. We then continue with the second value of attribute $A$, which is $b$, and intersect $b$'s attribute set $\{A, B\}$ with the respective candidates. Afterward, $A$'s set of referenced attributes is empty and BINDER stops processing this index entry, ignoring the values

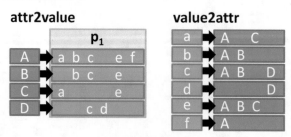

Figure 4.15: A dense *attr2value* index and an inverted *value2attr* index for an example partition $p_1$ with attributes {A,B,C,D} and values {a,b,c,d,e,f}.

Table 4.6: The checking process over the example indexes of Figure 4.15

| Loop Up | A B,C,D | B A,C,D | C A,B,D | D A,B,C |
|---|---|---|---|---|
| $A \to a \to$ A,C | **C** | A,C,D | **A** | A,B,C |
| $A \to b \to$ A,B | - | **A** | A | A,B,C |
| $B \to c \to$ A,B,D | - | **A** | A | **A,B** |
| $B \to e \to$ A,B,C | - | **A** | **A** | A,B |
| $D \to d \to$ D | - | A | A | - |

$c$, $e$, and $f$. The algorithm then continues with $B$, where the value $b$ is skipped as it has already been handled for $A$. After handling the values $c$ and $e$ with $B$ and the value $d$ with $D$, BINDER reports the two valid INDs $B \subseteq A$ and $C \subseteq A$. Note that the entry for $f$ was never tested in the *values2attr* index and, in real-world datasets, many values never have to be tested.

One important feature of the BINDER candidate validation strategy is that it also works for n-ary INDs with one small change: instead of bucketizing single attribute values, the algorithm bucketizes n-ary value combinations. To generate n-ary IND candidates, BINDER uses the same bottom-up lattice traversal strategy as the algorithm MIND (see Section 4.5.8). For most datasets, BINDER performs better than MIND due to its superior candidate validation. The algorithm, however, requires a lot of disk space to store all the buckets with n-ary value combinations.

### 4.5.5   SPIDER

In contrast to DEMARCHI and BINDER, SPIDER [Bauckmann et al., 2006] implements IND candidate validation using an all-column sort-merge join, a two-phase validation procedure that first sorts the input data column-wise and then joins all column pairs in one pass. Similar to DE-

MARCHI, however, SPIDER validates multiple IND candidates simultaneously via set-operations and, similar to BINDER, the algorithm prunes attributes that have been removed from all of their IND candidates.

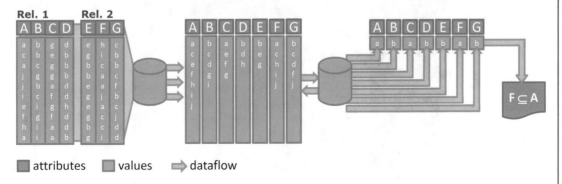

Figure 4.16: The sort and merge phases of the SPIDER algorithm by example.

Figure 4.16 illustrates the two-phase validation process of SPIDER. In the first phase, which is the *sort phase*, the algorithm sorts the values of each column and writes the sorted value lists to disk. Each such list of values is stored in a separate file. The proposed sorting strategy is to query one attribute at a time with an ORDER BY SQL statement. While this is arguably the easiest and also the most efficient implementation, it works only if the data resides in a relational database. If the data are read from a no-SQL source, the SPIDER algorithm needs to do the sorting (e.g., a *two-phase multiway merge sort*). To reduce the size of each sorted value list, the first phase removes duplicates.

In phase two, the *merge phase*, SPIDER first generates all possible IND candidates, similar to DEMARCHI and BINDER. Next, it opens all sorted value lists simultaneously and reads their first values into a priority queue, i.e., a queue of attribute-value pairs that is sorted by value. Figure 4.7 shows an example of such a priority queue. It then takes all attribute-value pairs with the same value from the top of the queue and puts their attributes into a set, e.g., {A,C,F} in our example. This set is equivalent to the same-value attribute sets in DEMARCHI and BINDER: all attributes in this set can be included in one another but not in other attributes. Then, SPIDER intersects this set with all IND candidates whose LHS attribute occurs in it (see Section 4.5.3 for an example). Since the value for this current same-value attribute set, i.e., "a" in our example, has now been handled, the algorithm discards the value and reads, for each attribute in the same-value attribute set, the next value from respective sorted value list. The new resulting attribute-value pairs are then inserted into the priority queue, from where the algorithm reads the next same-value attribute set. SPIDER continues until all files are read (or all IND candidates have been falsified). If an attribute has been removed from all of its IND candidates, SPIDER closes the pointers to its sorted value list, which effectively prunes this attribute from the validation process. In the end, only valid IND candidates survive the checking procedure.

Table 4.7: SPIDER's all-column merge phase to retrieve same-value attribute sets for unary IND candidate validation after the sorting phase. See Figure 4.16 for data.

| | Priority Queue | | | | | | |
|---|---|---|---|---|---|---|---|
| Value: | a | a | a | b | b | b | b |
| Attribute: | A | C | F | B | D | E | G |
| | ↳ {A,C,F} | | | | | | |
| Value: | b | b | b | b | c | c | e |
| Attribute: | B | D | E | G | A | F | C |
| | ↳ {B,D,E,G} | | | | | | |
| Value: | c | c | c | c | d | e | e |
| Attribute: | A | B | F | G | D | E | C |
| | ↳ {A,B,F,G} | | | | | | |
| Value: | d | d | d | e | e | e | h |
| Attribute: | B | D | G | A | C | E | F |
| | ↳ {B,D,G} | | | | | | |
| Value: | e | e | e | f | g | h | h |
| Attribute: | A | C | E | G | B | D | F |
| | ↳ {A,C,E} | | | | | | |
| | | | | ... | | | |

The SPIDER algorithm was published as a discovery algorithm for unary INDs only, but the extensions needed to also discover n-ary INDs are the same as for BINDER: use a candidate generation similar to MIND, which successively generates n-ary IND candidates from (n-1)-ary candidates, and use the sorting-based validation technique on attribute combinations rather than individual attributes.

SPIDER is easy to implement, especially when utilizing SQL for sorting, it is memory-efficient due to storing sorted value lists on disk, and its validation strategy is efficient. However, the need to sort the entire input dataset column-wise is a drawback when compared to BINDER because it is more expensive than hashing. Another point to consider is that most operating systems limit the number of simultaneously open file handles and SPIDER requires one such file handle per attribute.

## 4.5.6   S-INDD

S-INDD is a four-step approach to unary IND discovery that improves the SPIDER algorithm while borrowing some techniques from the BINDER algorithm [Shaabani and Meinel, 2015].

S-InDD uses an all-column sort-merge join, but with several performance optimizations. The novelty of this algorithm is that it avoids redundant set intersections during the candidate validation procedure.

A performance issue in DeMarchi, Binder, and Spider is that some set intersections are executed multiple times for different values. For example, assume that the attributes $A$, $B$, and $C$ all include the same $n$ values $v_1 \ldots v_n$. The three previous algorithms would form the same-value attribute list $\{A, B, C\}$ for each value, i.e., $n$-times, and intersect it with the IND candidates of $A$, $B$, and $C$. The S-InDD algorithm avoids these redundant intersections by pre-calculating all such same-value attribute lists, the so-called attribute *clusters*, and then deduplicating them. If the number of redundant intersections is high and if such lists are long, the overall intersection costs outweigh the deduplication costs and S-InDD outperforms Spider. This is typically the case for randomly generated datasets, log-stream data, and very large datasets in general; for small to medium sized datasets, S-InDD's deduplication costs usually exceed their gain.

In phase one, S-InDD reads the input data and pairs each value with its source attribute. Similar to Spider, S-InDD sorts these pairs lexicographically by their value, removes duplicate entries, and writes the resulting value-attribute pairs into separate lists $L_i$ to disk. Sorting can be done via SQL or within the S-InDD algorithm. Table 4.8 shows four such sorted lists of initial value-attribute pairs. Similar to the Binder algorithm, S-InDD splits these lists into multiple partitions such that each level of partitions holds all values with the same hash, and all further phases of S-InDD can operate level-wise on these partitions.

Table 4.8: Initial sorted lists of value-attribute pairs

| $L_1$ | (a,{A}) | (b,{A}) | (c,{A}) | (e,{A}) | (f,{A}) |
|---|---|---|---|---|---|
| $L_2$ | (b,{B}) | (c,{B}) | (e,{B}) | | |
| $L_3$ | (a,{C}) | (e,{C}) | | | |
| $L_4$ | (c,{D}) | (d,{D}) | | | |

In phase two, S-InDD merges some sorted lists. The assumption is that only $k$ files can be read simultaneously without exhausting the operating system limit on open file handles. Hence, the algorithm opens $k$ files, merges them into one file, again opens $k$ files merging them into one, and so on until only $k$ files remain; if there are only $k$ or fewer files initially, then no merge is needed. The merge procedure itself is similar to the generation of same-value attribute lists in Spider: collect all value-attribute pairs with the same value, merge the attributes, write the resulting value-attribute pairs to disk, read the next value from each sorted list, and collect the next round of equal values. If $k = 2$, the result of the merge phase in our example would be as shown in Table 4.9.

In phase three, the S-InDD algorithm opens the remaining $k$ sorted lists and collects the final attribute clusters, as in the Spider algorithm. As the actual value of each cluster is no

Table 4.9: Merged sorted lists of value-attribute tuples with $k = 2$

| $L_{1,2}$ | (a,{A}) | (b,{A,B}) | (c,{A,B}) | (e,{A,B}) | (f,{A}) |
|---|---|---|---|---|---|
| $L_{3,4}$ | (a,{C}) | (c,{D}) | (d,{D}) | (e,{C} | |

Table 4.10: The collected and deduplicated attribute clusters

| $L_{1,2,3,4}$ | {A} | {A,B} | {C} | {D} |
|---|---|---|---|---|

longer needed, S-INDD continues with attribute clusters alone. Instead of directly applying the clusters, S-INDD first stores and deduplicates them. The result is shown in Table 4.10.

In phase four, S-INDD uses only the remaining attribute clusters for candidate validation. In our example, this reduces the overall number of attribute set intersections from 12 (see Figure 4.8) to 5 (see Figure 4.10) when compared to the DEMARCHI algorithm that executes all intersections. When compared to BINDER and SPIDER, the reduction is from 6 to 4 intersections because these algorithms also prune intersections with the invalidation of their candidates.

### 4.5.7    SINDY

An alternative approach to speed up IND discovery is to massively parallelize or distribute the computation, such that each worker or thread processes a fragment of the input. The SINDY algorithm is one such approach that implements IND discovery as a MapReduce-like workflow [Kruse et al., 2015a]. The functional API that SINDY is based upon mimics the Java collection API with higher-order functions, such as `map`, `filter`, `reduce`, `join`, or `groupBy`. Although SINDY was originally designed for the Stratosphere[1] framework, its API requirements are also met by most modern batch/stream processing engines, such as Apache Spark,[2] Apache Flink,[3] or Apache Storm.[4]

Figure 4.17 visualizes the SINDY transformation pipeline for IND discovery with some example data. The first transformation reads the input data in parallel (e.g., from a distributed file system). The second transformation is a `flatMap` that maps each value to its attribute, similarly to what the S-INDD algorithm does in its first phase. Since all records can be mapped independently, SINDY can parallelize these operations. Next, the `groupBy` transformation groups all value-attribute pairs by their values, aggregates the attributes in each group into one list, and sends this list to the next transformation. The next transformation is a `flatMap` that generates, for each attribute set $X$, all possible unary IND candidates $A \subseteq X \setminus A$, i.e., it generates all pairs

---

[1]http://stratosphere.eu/
[2]https://spark.apache.org/
[3]https://flink.apache.org/
[4]http://storm.apache.org/

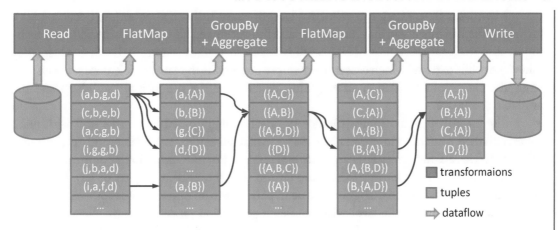

Figure 4.17: SINDY's transformation pipeline for IND discovery by example.

$(A, X \setminus A)$ for all $A \in X$. Again, each attribute set can be processed in parallel. The last transformation, groupBy, groups unary IND candidates by their left hand side attribute and intersects the right hand side attribute lists. The results are valid INDs, which are written to disk by the final write action.

SINDY includes further optimizations, e.g., the first flatMap transformation should pre-aggregate value-attribute pairs to reduce the communication overhead in the subsequent shuffle phase, and the final groupBy transformation should sort and deduplicate the attribute lists before intersecting them. However, the six-step transformation pipeline and its parallelization potential are the main reasons why SINDY can outperform other IND detection algorithms on large datasets when running on a cluster.

## 4.5.8 MIND

MIND is a breadth-first, bottom-up lattice traversal algorithm for discovering n-ary INDs with n > 1 [Marchi et al., 2009]. The algorithm assumes that all unary INDs are given, i.e., a unary IND discovery algorithm needs to be executed prior to MIND.

MIND uses a bottom-up candidate generation strategy that starts with the given unary INDs and proceeds level-wise to INDs of larger arity. To generate IND candidates of size n + 1, MIND uses a variation of the frequent itemset mining algorithm *apriori-gen* [Agrawal and Srikant, 1994]; it creates all IND candidates $X \subseteq Y$ of arity n + 1 whose direct generalizations of size n are *all* true INDs. More formally, an IND $X \subseteq Y$ with $|X| = |Y| = $ n + 1 is a candidate iff $\forall i \in [1, ..., n] : X \setminus X_i \subseteq Y \setminus Y_i$. This strategy follows from the fact that any generalization of a valid n-ary IND needs to be valid as well (see Section 4.1.3). If one such generalization is not contained in the set of n-ary INDs, all its specializations of size n + 1 can be pruned (upward-pruning).

MIND uses SQL queries to validate a level of n-ary IND candidates (see Section 4.5.1). However, the BINDER algorithm has shown that the optimized all-column join validation techniques also work for these n-ary IND candidate sets: instead of joining individual values, they join value combinations (which uses more memory but retains the same efficient validation strategy). The choice of a validation strategy thus depends on the number of candidates and the available disk space.

The breadth-first, bottom-up lattice traversal strategy of MIND works well with null values and their consistent interpretation. As we explained earlier, null values in LHS attributes of n-ary INDs can match any RHS attribute and null values in RHS attributes only match other null values. The algorithm must therefore ensure that the non-null part of any LHS value combination is included and can ignore the null part. Given an n-ary IND candidate, this check has already been done in the level-wise candidate generation process because all value subsets have been tested prior to the validation of the current candidate. For this reason, candidate validation can ignore any value combination that contains at least one null value. We already know that, for any n-ary value with nulls, the non-null part is included, and, since null can take any value from the RHS, the record cannot violate any IND candidate. Similarly, RHS values with nulls can be ignored because their null value on the RHS does not match any non-null LHS value and is therefore not needed for validation. Other lattice traversal algorithms that prune generalization checks require special null-value treatment in order to handle such values consistently.

### 4.5.9  FIND2

The FIND2 algorithm is a depth-first lattice traversal approach that generates n-ary IND candidates from hypergraphs [Koeller and Rundensteiner, 2003]. It assumes that many INDs are very large and therefore occur in high lattice levels. Finding such a large IND allows the algorithm to prune all its generalizations, i.e., all subset INDs, because these must be valid as well. Instead of increasing the arity of the generated candidates, FIND2 uses the given INDs to infer and then validate the largest possible INDs.

FIND2 models known INDs as $k$-uniform-hypergraphs. Each node represents a valid unary IND, e.g., $A \subseteq E, B \subseteq F, C \subseteq G$, and $D \subseteq H$ would be four nodes in a hypergraph. An edge in a $k$-uniform-hypergraph is a $k$-ary IND. For example, the edge $(A \subseteq E, B \subseteq F)$ represents the binary IND $AB \subseteq EF$ and the hyper-edge $(A \subseteq E, B \subseteq F, C \subseteq G, D \subseteq H)$ represents the 4-ary IND $ABCD \subseteq EFGH$. Given a $k$-uniform-hypergraph, i.e., one that holds all unary INDs as nodes and $k$-ary INDs as edges, inference of IND candidates with maximum arity is equivalent to the maximum clique finding problem. A clique of $x$ strongly connected nodes in a $k$-uniform-hypergraph describes an IND candidate of arity $x$ where all $k$-ary generalizations are valid INDs. Assume, for instance, that we find a clique of $x = 4$ nodes, which are $A \subseteq E, B \subseteq F, C \subseteq G$, and $D \subseteq H$. Then, we would derive the 4-ary IND candidate $ABCD \subseteq EFGH$. Depending on whether the clique contains binary or ternary hyperedges, we know that either all binary or ternary generalizations of $ABCD \subseteq EFGH$ are true. Thus, any $k$-uniform hypergraph lets the algorithm infer high arity INDs, but with larger $k$ the inferred candidates become more accurate, i.e., the likelihood of overestimating the size of a candidate is reduced.

Since the inference of IND candidates improves with larger $k$, i.e., with the arity of the given INDs, FIND2 takes not only the unary INDs but also INDs of higher arity—typically the first two to three lattice levels—as input. In practice, we would therefore run some unary IND discovery algorithm first, then the MIND algorithm for binary and ternary INDs, and finally FIND2 for the remaining INDs.

Finding maximum cliques in graphs is an NP-hard problem. To solve it in the context of IND discovery, FIND2 proposes the *hyper-clique* algorithm that performs well on sparse graphs with a small number of cliques [Koeller and Rundensteiner, 2002]. Given all INDs of up to some arity $k$, FIND2 first constructs the corresponding hypergraphs and identifies their cliques using *hyper-clique*. The cliques are then translated into IND candidates and validated using SQL. If a candidate is a true $x$-ary IND, FIND2 adds this edge to the corresponding $x$-uniform-hypergraph and prunes all its generalizations. If the candidate is false, FIND2 generates and validates all its $(x - 1)$-ary generalizations (top-down traversal). The algorithm terminates when all possible IND candidates have either been tested or pruned.

## 4.5.10 ZIGZAG

ZIGZAG uses a bi-directional lattice traversal approach that combines pessimistic bottom-up and optimistic top-down IND discovery [Marchi and Petit, 2003]. Given some low arity INDs, the idea is to estimate an optimistic positive border, which contains or at least is close to the maximal INDs, and then start two opposed lattice traversal processes: one *apriori-gen*-based breadth-first, bottom-up traversal process starting from the given INDs, and one breadth-first, top-down traversal process starting from the optimistic positive border, i.e., the pre-calculated upper bound in the lattice. Depending on the results of candidate validation, the ZIGZAG algorithm dynamically switches between the two traversal processes—it "zigzags" between bottom and top IND candidates.

Similar to FIND2, ZIGZAG takes unary INDs and INDs of larger arity as input. This improves the estimation of the optimistic positive border. ZIGZAG then initializes two IND sets: the negative border $Bd^-$ to store all minimal NON-INDs and the positive border $Bd^+$ to store all maximal valid INDs. The two sets store only minimal and maximal dependencies, respectively. Negative and positive borders are used for candidate pruning; all specializations of NON-INDs in $Bd^-$ are also NON-INDs and all generalizations of INDs in $Bd^+$ are also valid INDs.

The next step in the ZIGZAG algorithm is to estimate the optimistic positive border $oBd^+$. This border is a set of high-arity IND candidates that are not violated by any NON-IND in $Bd^-$. In other words, no IND candidate in $oBd^+$ has a generalization in $Bd^-$. To estimate the initial candidates for $oBd^+$, the algorithm infers high-arity IND candidates from the given low-arity INDs using inference rules from related work [Demetrovics and Thi, 1995], inter alia those from the FIND2 algorithm.

Once the initial optimistic border has been fixed, ZIGZAG evaluates all candidates in this border. Whenever a candidate is valid, the algorithm adds the discovered IND to the positive border $Bd^+$ and prunes all its generalizations; otherwise the resulting NON-IND is added to the negative border and all its specializations are pruned. For any NON-IND, ZIGZAG also calculates the corresponding $g_3'$ error, which specifies the percentage of records that violate the IND [Lopes et al., 2002]. If this error is small, then it is very likely that some specialization(s) of the current NON-IND is true. For this reason, ZIGZAG compares the error to some threshold and, if the error is below that threshold, it creates and validates the generalizations of the current NON-IND.

When all candidates in $oBd^+$ have been validated, ZIGZAG switches to the bottom-up traversal strategy. By downward pruning, some candidates should have been pruned already. After validating the next level of candidates, the algorithm again estimates a new optimistic border and returns to candidate validation. In this way, ZIGZAG approaches maximal INDs from both sides. When all candidates have been validated, $Bd^+$ contains the final result and the algorithm terminates.

ZIGZAG uses SQL queries for candidate validation. In contrast to other IND discovery approaches, ZIGZAG calculates the $g_3'$ error and therefore cannot leverage early termination. Depending on the number and positioning of maximal INDs in the lattice, the algorithm still competes well with the other approaches.

### 4.5.11 MIND2

MIND2 is an alternative IND discovery algorithm that, instead of checking individual IND candidates, searches for n-ary INDs via comparison of value coordinates and successive candidate refinement [Shaabani and Meinel, 2016]. It is a dependency induction algorithm, such as the FD discovery algorithm FDEP, although MIND2's comparison strategies for IND discovery differ from those proposed for FD discovery. Despite the name similarity, MIND2 has little in common with MIND. As input, MIND2 expects all unary INDs.

The fundamental data structures in MIND2 are *unary* IND *coordinates* or *coordinates* for short. A coordinate is a pair of integers $(i, j)$ that indicates for a specific unary IND $A \subseteq B$ that the value at record index $i$ in the LHS attribute $A$ is the same as the value at record index $j$ in the RHS attribute $B$. Each unary IND $A \subseteq B$ therefore describes a set of such coordinates $C_{A \subseteq B}$, which is defined as $C_{A \subseteq B} = \{(i, j) | r_i[A] = r_j[B]\}$ with records $r_i$ and $r_j$. By combining the coordinates in these sets, MIND2 can check, for every LHS record index $i$, which maximal n-ary INDs this position allows. Given that, for instance, all three unary INDs $A \subseteq D$, $B \subseteq E$, and $C \subseteq F$ and only these three INDs contain the same coordinate $(i, j)$, they form—just by looking at position $i$—the maximal n-ary IND candidate $ABC \subseteq DEF$. The coordinate $(i, j)$ indicates that some value combination in $ABC$ at index $i$ also occurs in $CDE$ at index $j$.

MIND2 derives maximal INDs from unary IND coordinates and gradually refines a set of n-ary INDs. First, MIND2 calculates the coordinate sets $C_u$ for every unary IND $u$, thus, is similar to the S-INDD and SPIDER algorithm, i.e., MIND2 queries the individual columns in sorted order, joins these columns on every input IND, and retains only the indexes $i$ and $j$ of every joined record pair. All coordinates are written to disk, one file per coordinate set $C_u$. Due to the sort-merge join procedure, these coordinate sets are automatically sorted by LHS index $i$.

Once all $C_u$ are created, MIND2 defines the set $I_M$ to store all maximal n-ary INDs and initializes this set to the most specialized n-ary IND possible, which is the composition of all unary INDs. Next, the algorithm opens all $C_u$ files simultaneously. It then reads all coordinates with the same first $i$ index from every $C_u$ file and groups these coordinates by their $j$ index. As explained above, each group describes a maximal IND candidate for the current position $i$. From the derived maximal IND candidates, MIND2 selects only those that are also maximal w.r.t. the entire set of derived maximal IND candidates of the current position. The reasoning for this maximization is that value combinations with null values can generate IND candidates that are non-maximal. The algorithm then intersects the maximal INDs in $I_M$ with the derived maximal INDs of position $i$ to refine $I_M$, i.e., it intersects all pairs of derived and $I_M$ INDs. Now that the current LHS index $i$ has been handled, MIND2 reads the next set of coordinates with $i + 1$ from the $C_u$ files to, again, find the maximal IND candidates and use them to refine $I_M$. By successively processing coordinates with increasing LHS index $i$, $I_M$ always contains the truly maximal INDs up this index. Once all $C_u$ files are read, $I_M$ is returned as the final result.

The algorithm becomes more complex if we consider null values because null values do not generate unary IND coordinates. Hence, if a $C_u$ set is missing a coordinate for some LHS index $i$, it needs to be treated as a coordinate that matches any RHS index.

In summary, MIND2 is an alternative approach for n-ary IND discovery. It does not necessarily rely on SQL (although the published version uses SQL for generating IND coordinates), requires only unary INDs as input, and has been shown to outperform FIND2 on certain datasets. However, MIND2 also has some shortcomings: if the number of unary INDs is large, the algorithm might not be able to open all $C_u$ files simultaneously due to operating system limitations on open file handles; unary INDs with only a few distinct values in their LHS and RHS attributes may also generate many coordinates, i.e., in the worst case, both columns contain only one value so that their join generates a quadratic number of coordinates; and, like BINDER, MIND2 requires additional disk space for storing intermediate data.

CHAPTER 5

# Relaxed and Other Dependencies

In the previous chapter, we discussed three important column dependencies: unique column combinations, functional dependencies, and inclusion dependencies. Furthermore, we have considered only those dependencies that hold without any exceptions. We now survey other kinds of dependencies.

A common way to define new dependencies is to relax the requirements of existing dependencies. As mentioned in Caruccio et al., we can relax the *extent* to which the dependency holds (it may hold on some subset of tuples but be violated by other tuples) or we can relax the corresponding *attribute comparison* (e.g., two values may satisfy a dependency if they are similar but not necessarily equal) [Caruccio et al., 2016].

The extent of a dependency can be relaxed either through syntactic conditions, which restrict the scope of a dependency to certain records that match the condition, or through coverage measures, which specify the fraction of records that must satisfy the dependency. This motivates new algorithms to discover such *conditional* and *partial* dependencies, respectively.

The attribute comparison relaxation can also be done in two ways: through *approximate matching* of values, i.e., similarity or semantic matching instead of equality, or considering *order*, usually lexicographical or numerical value order, instead of equality. Note that value equality is a special case of both attribute comparison relaxations, representing perfect similarity and total order.

In this chapter, we explain the different types of relaxed dependencies and point out their applications. Furthermore, we discuss approximate dependencies and we survey additional types of dependencies that are not formulated using the above relaxation patterns.

## 5.1 RELAXING THE EXTENT OF A DEPENDENCY

A functional dependency $X \rightarrow Y$ asserts that no two tuples can have different values of $Y$ if they have the same value of $X$. Relaxing the extent of an FD allows some tuples to not satisfy this requirement. The exclusion can be explicitly encoded through a syntactic condition or implicitly by tolerating a certain number of violating tuples. As we will discuss below, these relaxations lead to new challenges for the corresponding discovery algorithms.

## 5.1.1  PARTIAL DEPENDENCIES

A *partial* dependency holds only for a subset of the data [Abedjan et al., 2015b]. For example, in Table 5.1, first → last is a partial FD that is violated by tuple-pair (2,3) but satisfied by all other tuple pairs.

Table 5.1: Example dataset with partial FD first → last

| Tuple ID | First | Last | Age | Phone |
|----------|-------|-------|-----|-------|
| 1 | Max | Payne | 32 | 1234 |
| 2 | Eve | Smith | 24 | 5432 |
| 3 | Eve | Payne | 24 | 3333 |
| 4 | Max | Payne | 24 | 3333 |

Formally, a partial dependency $X \vdash_{\Psi \leq \varepsilon} Y$ is valid iff the error $\Psi$ of $X \vdash Y$ is smaller or equal than a given threshold $\varepsilon$ [Caruccio et al., 2016]. A partial dependency is minimal iff all its generalizations (or specializations for INDs) exceed the error threshold. Partial dependencies are useful if the data are expected to contain errors which would otherwise invalidate them and therefore hide potentially meaningful column relationships. A popular error measure is *the minimum number of records that must be removed to make the partial dependency exact* [Huhtala et al., 1999], but there are also ways to measure the error rate [Caruccio et al., 2016, Kivinen and Mannila, 1995]. Note that prior work such as Huhtala et al. [1999] and Marchi et al. [2009] does not explicitly distinguish between approximate and partial dependencies. In this book, approximate dependencies are those which hold with a certain probability while partial dependencies hold if a bounded number of records is removed.

Typically, any dependency discovery algorithm such as TANE or HYFD can be configured to detect partial dependencies. The implementation simply has to adjust the validation definition to incorporate the error rate $\Psi$. Furthermore, Kruse and Naumann present a new framework based on a so-called separate-and-conquer search strategy for discovering partial UCCs and partial FDs [Kruse and Naumann, 2018]. A particular challenge in partial FDs is that it becomes harder to decide the usefulness of the discovered FDs. In particular, there is a trade-off between minimality and coverage. For example, a minimal partial FD might have a higher error rate than the same FD with more attributes on the left-hand side.

## 5.1.2  CONDITIONAL DEPENDENCIES

A *conditional* dependency, such as a conditional IND [Bravo et al., 2007] or a conditional FD [Fan et al., 2008b], is a partial dependency that explicitly specifies conditions that restrict its scope. Conditions are typically sets of *pattern tuples* that summarize satisfying tuples. The set of pattern tuples is called a *pattern tableau* or simply a *tableau* [Bohannon et al., 2007].

Formally, a conditional dependency is a pair $(X \vdash Y, T_p)$, that includes an underlying dependency $X \vdash Y$ and a pattern tableau $T_p$. The pattern tableau $T_p$ is a set of tuples $t \in T_p$ where each $t[A]$ with $A \in X \cup Y$ is either a constant or wildcard [Bravo et al., 2007]. Pattern tableaux identify syntactic conditions for satisfying tuples and therefore describe which parts of the data satisfy the underlying dependency (with the remaining parts containing errors with respect to the dependency).

To illustrate conditional functional dependencies (CFDs), recall Table 5.1. Here, {first,last} → age does not hold on the entire relation, but it holds on a subset of it where first = Eve. Formally, a CFD consists of two parts: an embedded FD $X \rightarrow A$ and an accompanying *pattern tuple* with attributes $XA$. Each cell of a pattern tuple contains a value from the corresponding attribute's domain or a wildcard symbol "_". A pattern tuple identifies a subset of a relation instance in a natural way: a tuple $r_i$ matches a pattern tuple if it agrees on all of its non-wildcard attributes. In the above example, we can formulate a CFD with an embedded FD {first,last} → age and a pattern tuple (Eve, _, _), meaning that the embedded FD holds only on tuples that match the pattern, i.e., those with first = Eve. The *support* of a pattern tuple is defined as the fraction of tuples in $r$ that it matches, e.g., the support of (Eve, _, _) in Table 5.1 is $\frac{2}{4}$.

Special cases that resemble instance-level association rules are referred to as *constant* CFDs. In this case, there are no wildcards. For example, the following (admittedly accidental) CFD holds on Table 5.1: age → phone with a pattern tuple (32, 1234). In other words, if age = 32 then phone = 1234.

Additionally, as was the case with traditional FDs, we can define approximate CFDs as those CFDs that hold only partially on the tuples specified by the pattern tableau. To assess how often a CFD holds, *confidence* has been defined as the minimum number of tuples that must be removed to make the CFD hold. Based on this definition, several algorithms have been proposed for computing summaries that allow the confidence of a CFD to be estimated with guaranteed accuracy [Cormode et al., 2009].

Discovering conditional dependencies is more difficult than discovering exact, approximate, and partial dependencies [Diallo et al., 2012]; in addition to discovering the underlying dependency, we must also discover the pattern tableaux or pattern tuples. In fact, even finding one *optimal* tableau for one partial FD is NP-hard [Golab et al., 2008].

Discovery algorithms for conditional dependencies are usually based on the discovery algorithms for their exact counterparts. In conditional functional dependency discovery, for example, CTANE [Fan et al., 2011] and the algorithm from [Chiang and Miller, 2008] extend TANE and CFUN, CFD_MINER, and FASTCFDs [Diallo et al., 2012] are based on FUN, FD_MINE, and FASTFDs, respectively.

## 5.2  RELAXING ATTRIBUTE COMPARISONS

The standard attribute comparison method in dependency discovery is the equality comparison. For example, an FD $X \to Y$ holds if for the same value in $X$ we have no *unequal* values in $Y$. In some use cases, it might be desirable to expand the equality comparison in a way that semantically equal values can be tolerated as well. For example, a data owner might want to tolerate having "US" and "USA" as country names in a database without violating the FD area code $\to$ country. Hence, the dependency needs to relax the comparison operation on country names. Caruccio et al. identify 16 different types of comparison methods [Caruccio et al., 2016]. We summarize them as follows: the comparison method can either be relaxed on a value level, as is the case with *metric* or *matching* dependencies, or on the ordering level, as is the case with order and sequential dependencies.

### 5.2.1  METRIC AND MATCHING DEPENDENCIES

*Metric dependencies* relax the comparison method in a way that tolerates formatting differences. The main property of metric dependencies is that the relaxation has to be defined as a metric that satisfies symmetry and the triangle inequality. There is some existing work on the discovery of metric functional dependencies [Koudas et al., 2009].

Another line of research expresses a similar relaxation as *neighborhood dependencies* [Bassée and Wijsen, 2001]. A closeness function is defined for the Lʜs and Rʜs attributes. For example, the relaxed functional dependency *age→salary* would hold for all persons in a database as long as the age and salary are similar within some thresholds. A similar concept is known as a *differential dependency*. This relaxed dependency uses a differential function for each attribute in the form of a constraint. An example of a differential dependency is again the FD *age→salary* with the requirement that the salary difference of two persons must be within some bounds according to their age difference, i.e., if the age difference is 2 years then the salary difference must not be higher than 200 USD. Note that the bounds in differential dependencies can be variable, while the threshold in neighborhood dependencies is fixed.

Finally, it is possible to generalize these functions to more sophisticated patterns. The literature on *similarity* [Baixeries, 2012] and *fuzzy* [Bosc et al., 1994] dependencies explores the formal aspects of these kinds of dependencies. There is also some work on the so-called *Type-M* functional dependencies that define formal concepts on multimedia datasets [Chang et al., 2007]. Typically, more than one similarity metric has to be combined in order to identify the similarity of multi-media objects.

A metric dependency can be generalized to a *matching dependency*. A matching dependency (MD) $\phi$ is written as $R_1[X_1] \approx R_2[X_2] \to R_1[Y_1] \approx R_2[Y_2]$. It states that if any two records $t_1$ and $t_2$ from instances of $R_1$ and $R_2$, respectively, are pairwise similar in all $X$ attributes, they are also pairwise similar in all $Y$ attributes. While metric dependencies are defined based on syntactic similarity measures, such as Jaccard similarity, matching dependencies allow more general matching functions. First introduced by Fan [2008], MDs are formally defined as follows.

**Definition 5.1   Matching dependency.**   Given two relational instances $r_1$ and $r_2$ of schemata $R_1$ and $R_2$, respectively, a *matching dependency* $\phi$, written as $\bigwedge_{i \in [1,k]} \{R_1[X_1[i]] \approx_i R_2[X_2[i]]\} \to \bigwedge_{j \in [1,l]} \{R_1[Y_1[j]] \approx_j R_2[Y_2[j]]\}$ with $X_n \subseteq R_n$, $Y_n \subseteq R_n$, and attribute specific similarity operators $\approx_m$. $\phi$, is *valid* in $r_1$ and $r_2$ iff $\forall t_{1,p} \in r_1, t_{2,q} \in r_2 : \bigwedge_{i \in [1,k]} \{t_{1,p}[X_1[i]] \approx_i t_{2,q}[X_2[i]]\} \Rightarrow \bigwedge_{j \in [1,l]} \{t_{1,p}[Y_1[j]] \approx_j t_{2,q}[Y_2[j]]\}$.

Matching dependencies generalize functional dependencies in two ways: they extend the definition from one to two tables and they relax the comparison operator from strictly equal $=$ to similar $\approx$. Thus, a functional dependency is a matching dependency with $R_1 = R_2$ and $\approx$ being $=$ for all attributes.

Including two relations, $R_1$ and $R_2$, requires a one-to-one mapping of $X$ and $Y$ attributes. This means that $|X_1| = |X_2| = k$ and $|Y_1| = |Y_2| = l$. Thus, MD discovery algorithms either require a predefined attribute mapping or they consider all possible attribute mappings (with attributes having the same domain/datatype) for generating MD candidates.

The similarity operators $\approx$ specify a *similarity metric* for each pair of attributes, e.g., using numeric, edit, q-gram, time, or geo-distance, and a *similarity threshold*, i.e., a minimum similarity down to which values are considered similar. While the similarity metric depends on the domain/datatype of the attribute pair, the threshold depends on the data and needs to be discovered with the MDs. The thresholds may need to be small on the Lhs to match many tuples (the MD holds for any larger Lhs threshold anyway), and large on the Rhs up to the point that a larger value would invalidate the MD (the MD also holds for all smaller Rhs thresholds). Picking the right thresholds per dataset is an open problem. A possible direction is to learn the threshold from samples of the dataset.

The *matching operator* $\rightleftharpoons$ is a special form of the similarity operator $\approx$ that does not specify a metric or a threshold. It indicates that the values of two attributes match, i.e., refer to the same object, regardless of how different they actually are. Matching operators in MDs are found via implication analysis and generic reasoning about MDs that are already known.

To illustrate matching dependencies, consider the relational instances shown in Tables 5.2 and 5.3. Both instances store address data for restaurants and satisfy the following MDs.

1. *tel* $\approx_{Jaro,0.9}$ *phone* $\wedge$ *street* $\approx_{Levenshtein,0.6}$ *location* $\to$ *name* $\rightleftharpoons$ *label*.

2. *name* $\approx_{Levenshtein,0.7}$ *label* $\wedge$ *city* $=$ *town* $\to$ *tel* $\rightleftharpoons$ *phone*.

The first MD states that if telephone numbers and street values are sufficiently similar, i.e., 90% and 60%, respectively, then restaurant names should match. The matching here implies that the two values for name and label should be equal, but we can tolerate differences in the Lhs values because the value representation might differ in the two relations.

Table 5.2: An example instance for the schema Restaurant(name, tel, street, city, foot)

|  | Name | Tel | Street | City | Foot |
|---|---|---|---|---|---|
| $t_1$ | Aina Bar | 12-345 | Oktober St. | Berlin | Singaporean |
| $t_2$ | Jerry's Inn | 00-000 | Hill Ave. | New York | Mexican |
| $t_3$ | Katsu Y. | 42-911 | Katsu Ln. | Tokyo | Sushi |

Table 5.3: An example instance for the schema Eatery(label, phone, location, town, stars)

|  | Label | Phone | Location | Town | Stars |
|---|---|---|---|---|---|
| $t_1$ | Aina Bar | 12345 | Oktober St. 8 | Berlin | 1 |
| $t_2$ | Star Cafe | 01357 | Main St. 173 | Paris | 5 |
| $t_3$ | Katsu Yamo | 42911 | Katsu Ln. 1 | Tokyo | 4 |

The second MD states that if restaurant names are similar and the city is the same, then telephone numbers should match. The intuition behind this MD could be that restaurants names are well distinguishable within the same city so that different telephone numbers for similar restaurant names are probably data errors.

Matching functions are more prominent in works on record linkage. For example, matching records should correspond to the same real-world entity across different relations. Song and Chen [2009] published a first discovery algorithm for matching dependencies that proposes a successive validation method for MD candidates. Given an MD candidate, the algorithm lowers the candidate's Lhs similarity thresholds until predefined minimum support and confidence values are met; the Rhs similarity thresholds are decreased as needed, but if they become too small, meaning that nearly all values are considered similar, the MD candidate must be discarded. The discovery algorithm also uses pruning rules and approximation techniques to cope with the complexity of the MD discovery problem. In the end, however, the algorithm finds only a subset of valid MDs. The automatic discovery of a complete set of exact MDs is an open research question.

Finally, another way to relax the comparison operator is to add new dimensions such as ontological [Baskaran et al., 2017] and temporal relationships [Wijsen, 2009].

An ontology FD checks whether two values have the same meaning according to their relationship within an ontology. For example, if an ontology contains a sameAs relationship between concepts, such as "organization," "institution," and "management," these values would be considered equal. As a result, tuples that agree on the Lhs attribute(s) but have these three values in the Rhs attribute would not violate the dependency. This relationship can be either a synonym relationship or an inheritance relationship. In contrast to traditional FDs or variations of metric FDs, ontology FDs do not satisfy the triangle inequality.

Temporal dependencies allow different RHS values for the same LHS in different time-periods. For example, the dependency *person → location* might not be true in an event-tracking dataset because people move over time. However, if we add time $t$ to the LHS, we get *person, t →location*, which might hold. There are different ways of expressing time as part of a dependency such as an FD. One could use the timestamp, a discrete interval $I$ as suggested by Wijsen [2009], or the minimum expected duration of the rule as suggested by Abedjan et al. [2015a]. The notion of minimum expected duration arises from the fact that due to data sparsity, exact timestamps or intervals might not always be available. As shown by Abedjan et al. [2015a] facts extracted by web event extractors require a post-processing step to assess whether certain relationships and FDs have been correctly extracted. For this purpose, the corresponding expected durations need to be mined to verify whether the individual event information, such as *person → location*, are valid within the minimum expected duration.

## 5.2.2   ORDER AND SEQUENTIAL DEPENDENCIES

The aforementioned attribute comparison techniques focus on tuple values and similarity functions defined on strings. A different class of dependency relaxation is based on attribute comparisons that focus on the ordering of values. The most common example is the order dependency [Szlichta et al., 2017]. Order dependencies hold between columns as long as the ordering of both columns is aligned or inversely aligned. An *order dependency* (OD) is written as $X \to_\theta Y$. It states that if we sort the records w.r.t the attributes $X$ and some comparison operator $\theta$, then the records are also sorted w.r.t. the attributes $Y$ and $\theta$. Note that $X$ and $Y$ denote ordered attribute *lists* for ODs and not unordered attribute sets such as for UCCs or FDs. Order dependencies are useful for many tasks, such as integrity checking, index construction, and query optimization. In distributed message passing systems, they are particularly useful for detecting packet loss and for message reordering on the receiving side. A formal definition of order dependencies is given below.

**Definition 5.2  Order dependency.**    Given a relational instance $r$ of schema $R$, an *order dependency* $X \to_\theta Y$ with $X \subseteq R$, $Y \subseteq R$ and $\theta \in \{\leq, <, =, >, \geq\}$ is *valid* in $r$ iff $\forall t_i, t_j \in r$ : $t_i[X] \, \theta \, t_j[X] \Rightarrow t_i[Y] \, \theta \, t_j[Y]$.

Table 5.4 shows an example relation for a schema on Planets. This relation satisfies the two ODs sun_distance $\to_\theta$ temperature and temperature $\to_\theta$ sun_distance for all $\theta \in \{\leq, <, =, >, \geq\}$, meaning that if Planets is sorted by one of these attributes, it is also sorted by the other. In this example, the other attribute is sorted inversely as temperature decreases with the distance to the sun.

An order dependency with $\theta$ equal to $=$ is a functional dependency, meaning that the definition of ODs generalizes FDs. It has been proven that any order dependency $X \to_\leq Y$

Table 5.4: An example instance of the schema Planet(name, mass, sun_distance, gravity, temperature)

| | Name | Mass $10^{24}\,kg$ | Sun-distance $10^6\,km$ | Gravity $m/s^2$ | Temperature $Celsius$ |
|---|---|---|---|---|---|
| $t_1$ | Venus | 4.87 | 108.2 | 8.9 | 464 |
| $t_2$ | Earth | 5.97 | 149.6 | 9.8 | 15 |
| $t_3$ | Mars | 0.64 | 227.9 | 3.7 | -65 |
| $t_4$ | Jupiter | 1898.00 | 778.3 | 23.1 | -110 |
| $t_5$ | Saturn | 568.00 | 1427.0 | 9.0 | -140 |
| $t_6$ | Uranus | 86.80 | 2871.0 | 8.7 | -195 |
| $t_7$ | Neptune | 102.00 | 4497.1 | 11.0 | -200 |
| $t_8$ | Pluto | 0.013 | 5913.0 | 0.7 | -225 |

is also a functional dependency $X \to Y$, i.e., *order* is a special functional relationship [Szlichta et al., 2017]. However, the reverse is not true because functional dependencies do not imply order.

Order dependencies were first studied in Ginsburg and Hull [1983]. The works of Ng [2001] and Szlichta et al. [2012] then studied order dependencies and, in particular, lexicographical orderings in further detail. These works also provide a sound and complete axiomatization for ODs. In Szlichta et al. [2013], the authors propose techniques for OD inference from relational data and also prove that inference is co-NP-complete.

There are two algorithms for OD discovery: ORDER [Langer and Naumann, 2016] and FASTOD [Szlichta et al., 2017, 2018]. Both algorithms use a lattice-based bottom-up search strategy similar to TANE, but with OD candidate generation and OD pruning rules. ORDER validates candidate ODs using PLIS with *sorted partitions* w.r.t. the comparison operator $\theta$. Because the order of *all* partitions is relevant for OD validation, ORDER does not strip partitions of size one from the PLIS. To verify whether $X$ and $Y$ produce the same ordering, it suffices to scan through $\pi_X$ and $\pi_Y$ and ensure that there are no *swaps*, i.e., $t_1[X] < t_2[X]$ but $t_1[Y] > t_2[Y]$, or *merges*, i.e., $t_1[X] \neq t_2[X]$ but $t_1[Y] = t_2[Y]$.

In contrast, FASTOD maps list-based ODs into equivalent set-based canonical ODs. This allows FASTOD to traverse a significantly smaller search space which results in lower runtimes. Once discovered, the set-based ODs can be used to infer all list-based ODs (we do not discuss the inference rules here and instead refer the interested reader to Szlichta et al. [2017]). Using set-based ODs has further advantages: validating set-based ODs can be done over *stripped* partitions which can be significantly smaller; the set-based representation is more concise, consuming less memory; and additional pruning rules such as key pruning can be used during lattice traversal.

Order dependencies have been generalized to *sequential dependencies*. A sequential dependency, abbreviated SD, states that when sorted on $X$, any two consecutive values of $Y$ must be within a specific range. This is useful, for instance, to detect message loss in a network. Assume $X$ is a sequence number and $Y$ is time. Suppose thats the time gap between two consecutive messages, ordered by sequence number, should be at most 30 sec. In other words, we expect at least one message every 30 sec. Now suppose that we see two consecutive messages 60 sec apart (when sorted by sequence number). This means that a message must have been lost. Sequential dependencies as well as their approximate and conditional versions have been introduced in Golab et al. [2009]. The general problem of SD discovery is an open topic.

## 5.3    APPROXIMATING THE DEPENDENCY DISCOVERY

An *approximate* or *soft* dependency relaxes the hard correctness constraint of an exact dependency as it usually only holds on a sample dataset or on an approximation of the dataset such as a sketch [Ilyas et al., 2004]. In other words, an approximate algorithm has been used to discover the dependencies without guaranteeing correctness. This means that violations might exist in the data, and their number and location is unknown. However, in some scenarios, it is possible to guess the confidence of an approximate dependency or to state a certain worst-case confidence. For example, the approximate IND discovery algorithm FAIDA [Kruse et al., 2017b] was found to classify candidates as non-INDs with a confidence of 100% (because it does not produce false negatives), and as true INDs with an empirical confidence of 100% (because the algorithm did not produce a single false positive in any experiment with their proposed accuracy configuration). As the correctness of FDs is relaxed in approximate discovery, one can apply more efficient algorithms [Kivinen and Mannila, 1995]. Common techniques for approximate dependency discovery are sampling [Brown and Hass, 2003, Ilyas et al., 2004] and summarization [Bleifuß et al., 2016, Cormode et al., 2011, Kruse et al., 2017b, Zhang et al., 2010]. Note that a *set of dependencies* is called approximate if it approximates the completeness, correctness, and/or minimality of its elements [Bleifuß et al., 2016]. A more exhaustive discussion of dependency relaxation techniques can be found in the survey by Caruccio et al. [2016].

## 5.4    GENERALIZING FUNCTIONAL DEPENDENCIES

In the previous sections, we discussed various ways of relaxing a (functional) dependency. However, there are further ways of generalizing a dependency apart from relaxation. In this section, we discuss two generalizations of functional dependencies that refine the dependency definition using first-order logic statements (denial constrains) and statements over three instead of two records (multivalued dependencies). While denial constraints have found popularity in data cleaning applications, multivalued dependencies have been discussed in the context of schema normalization.

## 5.4.1   DENIAL CONSTRAINTS

A general approach to express various types of dependencies as business rules is the concept of *denial constraints*. Denial constraints (DCs) are a universally quantified first-order logic formalism, i.e., a rule language with certain predicates [Bertossi, 2011]. They describe value combinations that are forbidden, which is the opposite of how most other dependencies work, which is to specify constraints that must hold. Denial constraints can express functional and other dependencies. For example, the denial constraint $\forall t, t' : \neg(t[age] = t'[age] \wedge t[salary] \neq t'[salary])$ describes the functional dependency $age \rightarrow salary$ and the denial constraint $\forall t, t' : \neg(t[birthday] \leq t'[birthday] \wedge t[age] > t'[age])$ describes the order dependency $birthday \rightarrow_{\leq} age$. A formal definition of denial constraints is as follows.

**Definition 5.3   Denial constraint.**   Given a relational instance $r$ of schema $R$, a *denial constraint* is a negated conjunction of predicates written as a statement of the form $\forall t, t' :$ $\neg(u_1[A_1]\phi_1 v_1[B_1] \wedge \ldots \wedge u_k[A_k]\phi_k v_k[B_k])$ with tuples $u_i, v_i \in \{t, t'\}$, columns $A_i, B_i \in R$, and comparison operands $\phi_1 \in \{\leq, <, =, >, \geq\}$. It is valid in $r$ iff it is valid for all distinct tuples $t, t' \in r$.

A DC is trivial if it is valid for any possible instance of $R$ and it is (set-)minimal if no DC with a subset of its predicates is valid in $r$. Due to the expressiveness of denial constraints, they are particularly hard to discover. According to Szlichta et al. [2017], the search space for DCs contains $2^{12m(2m-1)}$, i.e., $O(2^{m^2})$ candidates for relations with $m$ attributes. These $2^{m^2}$ grow even faster than factorial $m!$.

The first discovery algorithm for denial constraints, FastDC, was published in Chu et al. [2013b]. It is inspired by FastFDs (see Section 4.4.6) and requires a similar comparison of all record pairs. Instead of agree-sets, FastDC calculates the set of satisfied predicates per record-pair and then derives the valid DCs in a second phase. In order to scale better with the number of records, the more recent algorithm Hydra [Bleifuß et al., 2017] avoids redundant comparisons of record-pairs that satisfy the same predicate set. For this purpose, Hydra combines a sampling of tuple pairs with a subsequent phase which ensures that all distinct predicate sets are found.

## 5.4.2   MULTIVALUED DEPENDENCIES

It is possible to extend dependencies by adding constraints on other columns or complementary relationships. One example is the *multivalued dependency*. A multivalued dependency (MVD) is written as $X \twoheadrightarrow Y$. It states that for some set of attributes $X$, there is another set of attributes $Y$ whose values are independent of all values in the remaining attributes $Z = R\backslash\{X \cup Y\}$. Such situations of value independence usually arise when joining two schemata $R_1 = XY$ and $R_2 = XZ$ on the attribute(s) $X$. For this reason, MVDs are often referred to as *join dependencies*. The value independence described by MVDs is mostly used for schema normalization: Given that $X \twoheadrightarrow Y$, split the schema $R = XYZ$ into $R_1 = XY$ and $R_2 = XZ$. If all MVDs are resolved this way, the schema fulfills the fourth normal form (4NF)—a successor of the well-known Boyce-Codd normal form (BCNF). Multivalued dependencies and 4NF were first defined by Fagin [1977]. MVDs and their use in schema normalization are well described in the database literature, see, e.g., Ullman [1990] and Garcia-Molina et al. [2008].

Another interesting property of MVDs, which stands in contrast to most other multi-column dependencies, is that their definition requires three tuples instead of two. UCCs check that every pair of tuples differs in certain values, FDs check that every pair with equal LHS values also has equal RHS values, and INDs check that every tuple with some LHS value finds a partner tuple with some RHS value; MVDs, in contrast, check that for each pair of tuples $t_i$ and $t_j$ that agree on their $X$ values, there is a third tuple $t_k$ that also agrees on $X$ and additionally agrees with $t_i$ on $Y$ and with $t_j$ on $Z$. The presence of such a $t_k$ ensures that the $Y$ values are independent of all other values for some specific $X$ value. More formally, multivalued dependencies are defined as follows.

**Definition 5.4    Multivalued dependency.**    Given a relational instance $r$ of a schema $R$, a *multivalued dependency* $X \twoheadrightarrow Y$ with $X \subseteq R$ and $Y \subseteq R$ is *valid* in $r$ iff $\forall t_i, t_j \in r : t_i[X] = t_j[X] \Rightarrow \exists t_k \in r : t_k[XY] = t_i[XY] \land t_k[R \backslash Y] = t_i[R \backslash Y]$.

Consider, for example, Table 5.5 that stores address data. It is common that one person has multiple addresses, i.e., a home and a family address, and multiple email accounts, i.e., one for private, work, and spam use. Because addresses and email accounts are independent, this example table produces two MVDs, namely *name* $\twoheadrightarrow$ *street, city* and *name* $\twoheadrightarrow$ *email, provider*. However, it does not contain any FDs and the only UCC contains all the attributes of the table.

Table 5.5: An example instance of schema Person(name, street, city, email, provider)

|       | Name      | Street       | City        | Email             | Provider  |
|-------|-----------|--------------|-------------|-------------------|-----------|
| $t_1$ | M. Walker | 42 Home St.  | Springfield | m.walker@uni.edu  | EDUCAUSE  |
| $t_2$ | M. Walker | 73 Work Ln.  | Franklin    | m.walker@uni.edu  | EDUCAUSE  |
| $t_3$ | M. Walker | 42 Home St.  | Springfield | mia87@gmail.com   | Gmail     |
| $t_4$ | M. Walker | 73 Work Ln.  | Franklin    | mia87@gmail.com   | Gmail     |
| $t_5$ | M. Walker | 42 Home St.  | Springfield | miwa123@aol.de    | AOL       |
| $t_6$ | M. Walker | 73 Work Ln.  | Franklin    | miwa123@aol.de    | AOL       |

Note that the definition of MVDs uses arbitrary pairs of tuples $(t_i, t_j)$ so that if it holds for $(t_1, t_2)$, it must also hold for $(t_2, t_1)$; the definition trivially holds for $(t_i, t_i)$. Another interesting detail about MVDs is that they generalize UCCs and FDs: $X \twoheadrightarrow Y$ holds if either $X$ is a UCC (because there are no two tuples $t_i$ and $t_j$ that agree on $X$) or $X \rightarrow Y$ is an FD (because $t_k = t_j$ always satisfies the MVD). However, in contrast to UCCs and FDs, MVDs always occur in pairs: if $X \twoheadrightarrow Y$ is a valid MVD, then $X \twoheadrightarrow Z$ with $Z = R\backslash\{X \cup Y\}$ is a valid MVD as well. This property is known as the *complementation rule*. More details on the interaction between FDs and MVDs as well as a set of inference rules for MVDs was given in Beeri et al. [1977]. Hartmann and Link later refined the set of inference rules in Hartmann and Link [2006].

Despite the research on MVD inference, there is little research on the efficient *discovery* of MVDs. MDEP, the first discovery algorithm for multivalued dependencies, was published in Flach and Savnik [1999] and Savnik and Flach [2000]. Similar to the FDEP algorithm for functional dependency discovery, the authors propose a dependency induction technique that first collects all non-MVDs in a negative cover and then inverts the negative cover into a set of minimal MVDs. The authors also discussed a bottom-up (in their lattice model top-down) approach that systematically generates and evaluates MVD candidates. Yan and Fu [2001] adapted the lattice-based FD discovery algorithm TANE to discover MVDs. They changed the search strategy, replaced the FD with MVD pruning rules, and discussed a validation method for MVD candidates based on partition refinement, i.e., position list indexes. Intuitively, an MVD candidate is valid iff for every equivalence class in $\pi_X$, the number of different $Y$ values times the number of different $Z$ values equals the size of the partition.

CHAPTER 6

# Use Cases

In this chapter, we take a closer look at the use cases of metadata, with a focus on dependencies: UCCs, FDs, and INDs. We also provide pointers for further reading about applications of other types of metadata.

Figure 6.1 provides an overview of popular use cases for data profiling and their interaction. The figure is not meant to be complete as further use cases (and types of metadata) exist. In general, data *preparation* use cases prepare data for ingest and analysis. Their purpose is to cleanse, shape, structure, integrate, and maintain data, and they are usually executed together or in some sequential order. Data *application* use cases generate business value, provide some insight, or enable some functionality. In contrast to the preparation uses cases, these do not aim to improve or maintain the data itself but rather make use of it. The remainder of this chapter discusses some of the illustrated use cases in more detail.

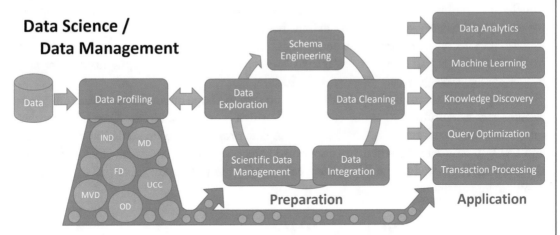

Figure 6.1: A visualization of various data science and data management use cases, their interaction, and their relationship with data profiling.

## 6.1 DATA EXPLORATION

Data exploration is the process of improving the understanding of the semantics and structure of a dataset. As such, data exploration involves a human who usually runs the process interactively. Johnson [2009] defines data profiling as "the activity of creating small but informative summaries of a database." Thus, the purpose of metadata is, by definition, to inform, create knowledge and extract insights.

Database administrators, researchers, and developers are often confronted with new and unfamiliar datasets. Examples include data files downloaded from the Web, old database dumps, or newly gained access to a DBMS. In many cases, such data have no known schema and no (or outdated) documentation. Even if a formal schema is specified, it might be incomplete, for instance specifying only the primary keys but no foreign keys.

A natural first step is to profile the data. Whenever a data scientist receives a new dataset, she may inspect its *format*, *schema*, *data types*, and some *example entries*. Then, she may measure the dataset's *size*, *length*, *width*, followed by *density* and *distribution of values* of certain attributes. This way, the data scientist develops a basic understanding of the data that allows her to effectively store, query, and manipulate it.

Further insights may be derived from complex dependencies. Recall the *ncvoter* dataset described in Chapter 4, which describes registered voters in the state of North Carolina. *Unique column combinations* describe attributes with special meaning, as these attributes uniquely identify each entity in the data. To uniquely identify a registered voter in North Carolina by first name and last name, one also needs the voter's birth year, phone number, registration date, and status, because these six attributes form a minimal UCC. With *functional dependencies*, we find additional structural laws and attributes with special relationships. For voters in North Carolina, for example, the birth year of a person defines her age. When used for data exploration, *inclusion dependencies* reveal relationships between different entities, for example, how voter records in the statewide registration list are related to voters in each city, i.e., city_raleigh.voter_id ⊂ ncvoter_statewide.voter_reg_num [Rostin et al., 2009].

Dependencies can also help discover relevant data in a large unfamiliar database. Discovery systems such as Aurum [Fernandez et al., 2018], which is embedded in the Data Civilizer data integration system [Deng et al., 2017], generate data profiles based on statistical distributions and INDs to represent the schema as a so-called enterprise knowledge graph (EKG). Based on the relationships stored in the EKG, users can identify tables that are related to each other or potential join attributes.

## 6.2    SCHEMA ENGINEERING

Schema engineering covers schema *reverse engineering* from data and schema *redesign*. Both tasks require metadata. Schema reverse engineering uses unique column combinations to rediscover keys [Saiedian and Spencer, 1996] and inclusion dependencies to identify foreign keys [Zhang et al., 2010]. Schema redesign can then use the UCCs, FDs, and INDs to interpret the schema as an entity-relationship diagram [Andersson, 1994]—a representation of the data that is easier to understand and manipulate than bare schema definitions in DDL statements.

A further subcategory of schema redesign is *schema normalization*. The goal of schema normalization is to remove redundancy in a relational instance by decomposing its relations into more compact relations. One popular normal form based on functional dependencies is the Boyce-Codd normal form (BCNF) [Codd, 1970]. In the normalization process, FDs represent the redundancy that is to be removed, whereas UCCs and INDs contribute keys and foreign keys [Zhang et al., 2010]. Several works, such as Bernstein [1976], Diederich and Milton [1988], Andritsos et al. [2004], or Papenbrock and Naumann [2017b], studied the algorithmic construction of a Boyce-Codd normal form using a dataset's FDs. An extension of BCNF is the Inclusion Dependency normal form (IDNF), which additionally requires INDs to be noncircular and key-based [Levene and Vincent, 1999].

## 6.3    DATA CLEANING

Data cleaning is the most popular use case of data profiling, which is why data cleaning tools include data profiling capabilities, e.g., Bellman [Dasu et al., 2002], Profiler [Kandel et al., 2012], Potter's Wheel [Raman and Hellerstein, 2001], and Data Auditor [Golab et al., 2010]. The general idea behind data cleaning with metadata is the same as for rule-based error detection systems: the metadata statements, which we can extract from the data, are rules, and records that contradict a rule are potential errors. To repair these errors, *equality-generating* dependencies, such as functional dependencies, enforce equal values of certain attributes if their records match in other attributes. On the other hand, *tuple-generating* dependencies, such as inclusion dependencies, enforce the existence of a tuple if some other tuple exists. In general, equality-generating dependencies govern data consistency and tuple-generating dependencies govern data completeness [Golab et al., 2011a].

*Exact* dependencies are not violated by any tuples. Thus, exact dependencies assume that the data are already clean and do not point out errors. In order to find dependencies in the presence of data errors, data scientists apply *approximate* or *partial* discovery algorithms, which allow some violations. If an approximate or partial dependency has been verified, i.e., it is said to be true despite having contradictions in some relational instance, then all violations must be data errors. A data cleaning process then resolves these errors, which are duplicate values in unique column combinations, mismatches in functional dependencies, missing values in inclusion dependencies, mismatches in multi-valued dependencies, order violations in order dependencies, or any denial constraint conflict. Data errors are repaired by correcting the offending values (making them equal or distinct) or correcting tuples (deleting contradicting tuples or generating missing tuples). Since there are often many ways to repair a dependency, we usually search for *minimal repairs* that resolve the violation(s) with a minimum number of edits.

Cleansing algorithms based on approximate dependencies usually discover the metadata from a (presumably clean) sample of records [Diallo et al., 2012]. Using partial dependencies, i.e., those for which we can specify the amount of tolerated contradictions, is more effective than using dependencies with unknown precision, but partial dependencies are also harder to discover. Most state-of-the-art approaches for metadata-based data cleaning, such as Bohannon et al. [2007], Fan [2008], and Dallachiesa et al. [2013b], use *conditional* metadata, i.e., metadata that explicitly counterbalance contradictions in the data with conditions. These conditions indicate errors and their scope [Cong et al., 2007]. The discovery of conditional statements is usually based on exact discovery algorithms, e.g., CTANE is based on TANE [Fan et al., 2011] and CFUN, CFD_MINER, and FastCFDs are based on FUN, FD_MINE, and FastFDs, respectively [Diallo et al., 2012]. Beyond conditional functional dependencies, we find cleaning tools, such as CLEANM [Giannakopoulou et al., 2017], that utilize denial constraints to check for errors in the data. Given some arbitrary first-order logic denial constraint statement, the tool identifies violations and suggests corrections.

The survey [Ilyas and Chu, 2015] presents a summary of data profiling and data cleaning. Besides approximate, partial, and conditional dependencies, they also advertise *denial constraints* for data cleaning. As described in Section 5.4.1, denial constraints are more expressive than most other types of dependencies. For this reason, they can easily express, among others, UCCs, FDs, ODs, their conditional variants, and more complex rules, such as *"For two employees, it should not be true that one has a higher salary, more working hours, and a lower final payment than the other."* Data cleaning frameworks, such as HoloClean [Rekatsinas et al., 2017], exploit the expressiveness of DCs for holistic data cleaning, which is, they translate all dependencies into DCs and search for the minimal number of data repairs to satisfy the entire set of DCs [Chu et al., 2013a].

A subtask of data cleaning is *integrity checking*. In this use case, dependencies identify missing and out-of-place records. For example, inclusion dependencies assure referential integrity [Casanova et al., 1988]. If an IND is violated, the data contains a record referencing a non-existent record so that either the first record is out of place or the second one is missing.

The relationship between data quality problems and metadata distribution is also a novel field of research. Visengeriyeva and Abedjan [2018] show that one can improve the performance of classifiers that detect data errors by using metadata as additional features.

Due to the importance of data quality in practice, there exist many data cleaning and repairing methods that use metadata. For a broader survey of such methods, we refer the reader to the work of Fan [2008].

## 6.4   QUERY OPTIMIZATION

Metadata can be used to optimize query execution. Query optimization primarily uses query plan rewriting and indexing [Chaudhuri, 1998]; it is extensively used in all modern database management systems. Query rewriting reformulates parts of queries with semantically equivalent but more efficient query terms [Gryz, 1999]. To illustrate the advantages of query rewriting, Figure 6.2 depicts the SQL query *"Find all Java developers by name that work on the backend of our website and already received a paycheck."*

The query joins the employee table with the paycheck table and outputs only those employees who received a paycheck. If we know that *all* employees received a paycheck, i.e., we

```
SELECT DISTINCT employee.name
FROM employee, paycheck
WHERE employee.ID = paycheck.employee
AND employee.expertise = `Java'
AND employee.workspace = `\product\backend';
```

Figure 6.2: Example SQL query that can be optimized with metadata.

know that the IND `employee.ID` $\subseteq$ `paycheck.employee` holds, then the join operation can be removed from the query [Gryz, 1998].

Now assume that {`employee.name`} is a UCC, i.e., no two employees have the same name. Then, the `DISTINCT` duplicate elimination is unnecessary. And if {`employee.expertise`} is another UCC, meaning that each employee has a unique expertise in the company, we can support the "Java"-expertise filter with an index on `employee.expertise` [Paulley and Larson, 1993].

Furthermore, we might find that the expertise of an employee defines her workspace. This would be reflected as an FD `employee.expertise` $\rightarrow$ `employee.workspace`. If the mapping "Java"-expertise to "backend"-workspace in the query is correct, then we can remove the "backend"-workspace filter [Paulley, 2000]. Even if we do not use the FD for query rewriting, the query optimizer should at least use this information to more accurately estimate the selectivity of the workspace filter whose selectivity is 1, i.e., no record is removed, because the expertise filter dominates the workspace filter.

```
SELECT employee.name
FROM employee
WHERE employee.expertise = `Java';
```

Figure 6.3: Example SQL query that was rewritten using metadata.

Figure 6.3 depicts the fully optimized query. Interestingly, it is irrelevant for this use case whether or not the metadata statements have semantic meaning; it is only important that they are valid at the time the query is asked. For this reason, exact data profiling results are directly applicable to query optimization.

## 6.5   DATA INTEGRATION

Data integration, also referred to as information integration, is the activity of matching different schemata and producing a joint representation [Bellahsene et al., 2011]. The matching part usually leads to a new, integrated schema that subsumes the important features of the initial schemata [Rahm and Bernstein, 2001]; this schema can also be a view [Ullman, 1997]. The main challenge in this process is to find correspondences between the individual schemata. These correspondences are difficult to find because attribute labels usually differ and expert knowledge for the different schemata is scarce [Kang and Naughton, 2003]. However, certain schema elements exhibit characteristic metadata signatures [Madhavan et al., 2001]. In fact, schema matching techniques, such as COMA [Do and Rahm, 2002], rely heavily on structural metadata, such as data types, statistics and dependencies. For instance, the foreign-key graph of schema $A$ may match the foreign-key graph of schema $B$ to some extent; a key of type integer with constant length 8 in schema $A$ may match with a key of type integer with constant length 8 in schema $B$; and a group of functionally dependent attributes in schema $A$ may have a counterpart in schema $B$ as well [Kang and Naughton, 2008].

A task related to data integration is *data linkage*. The goal of data linkage is not to merge but to connect schemata. This can be done by finding join paths and foreign key relationships between the different schemata. Because inclusion dependencies are able to indicate such relationships, they are critical for this task [Zhang et al., 2010].

CHAPTER 7

# Profiling Non-Relational Data

So far, we focused on profiling techniques for relational data with well defined datatypes and domains. This has also been the focus of the bulk of data profiling research. However, the "big data" phenomenon has not only resulted in more data but also in more types of data. Thus, profiling non-relational data is becoming a critical issue. In particular, the rapid growth of the World Wide Web and social networking has put an emphasis on graph data, semi-structured data such as XML and RDF and non-structured data such as text. In this chapter, we describe two types of solutions: those which apply traditional data profiling algorithms to new types of data and those which develop new approaches to profiling non-relational data.

## 7.1 XML

XML has been the standard for exchanging data on the Web, and many applications such as web services output their results as XML documents. Additionally, web services themselves are accessible through XML documents (e.g., WSDL, SOAP), which may be profiled to inspect and categorize web services. From a profiling point of view, the novelty of XML is that its structure explicitly contains useful mark-up and schema information.

Statistical analysis of XML documents focuses on the DTD structure, the XSD schema structure, and the inherent XML structure. In addition to element frequencies, XML statistics capture the "nestedness" of documents and element distributions at various nesting levels, e.g., the number of root elements and attributes and the depth of content nodes [Choi, 2002, Mignet et al., 2003, Mlynkova et al., 2006, Sahuguet and Azavant, 1999]. More complex approaches involve discovering traditional dependencies in XML data. Examples include extending the notion of, and discovering, FDs in XML data [Vincent et al., 2004], identifying redundancies based on the discovered FDs [Yu and Jagadish, 2006], and extending unique and key discovery to XML [Buneman et al., 2003]. Notably, due to the more relaxed structure of XML, these approaches identify approximate keys [Grahne and Zhu, 2002] or validate the identified keys against XSD definitions [Arenas et al., 2013].

As many XML documents do not refer to a specific schema, a relevant application of profiling is to support schema extraction [Bex et al., 2007, Hegewald et al., 2006]. Additionally, XML documents do not always follow syntactical rules [Korn et al., 2013], which may be identified via appropriate profiling techniques.

## 7.2   RDF

In general, XML profiling techniques are applicable to RDF datasets and vice versa. However, RDF profiling raises additional challenges due to the requirement that RDF needs to be machine readable and the important use case of Linked Open Data (LOD). Furthermore, there are many interesting RDF metadata elements beyond simple statistics and patterns of RDF statement elements; this includes synonymously used properties [Abedjan and Naumann, 2013], inverse relationships of properties, the conformity and consistence of RDF structured data to the corresponding ontology [Abedjan et al., 2012], and the distribution of literals and de-referenceable resource URIs from different namespaces.

LODStats is a recent stream-based tool that generates statistics about RDF datasets [Auer et al., 2012]. Also, ProLod++ is a tool for profiling RDF data using clustering and rule mining [Abedjan et al., 2014a]. Generally, there is a large body of work on mining RDF data and knowledge bases [Chen et al., 2016, Galárraga et al., 2015] for the purpose of knowledge discovery and ontology construction. Some of these approaches, such as AMIEE [Galárraga et al., 2015], can be used to mine information about the schema of an RDF dataset, but the main focus here is to generate new facts and knowledge rather than metadata (as intended in data profiling).

Because of the heterogeneity of interlinked sources, it is vital to identify where specific facts come from and how reliable they are. Therefore, an important task for profiling RDF data is provenance analysis [Böhm et al., 2011].

## 7.3   TIME SERIES

In general, a time series consists of an ordered sequence of elements, each element containing a timestamp or a sequence number that determines the ordering, as well as one or more associated numeric values. Time series datasets typically include multiple time series, each labeled, e.g., with the source of the data. For example, a mobility dataset may include location time series produced by smartphones. Each time series is labeled with the identifier of the smartphone that generated it, and each element contains the latitude and longitude (as well as a timestamp, of course). On the other hand, in finance, each time series may correspond to the stock price for a particular company.

Since time series are composed of numbers, profiling tasks for numeric columns apply. For instance, we can report the number of time series, the number of datapoints, the number of non-null or non-zero datapoints,[1] frequency histograms, and maximum and minimum values. Additionally, since each datapoint in a time series includes a timestamp or a sequence number, it is useful to report the timestamp or sequence number range and density (i.e., what time period did the measurements/values come from and how often were they generated/collected?).

---

[1]One should be careful when interpreting zeros in a time series as they may indicate missing data or correctly reported zero data (e.g., zero degrees temperature reported by a sensor or zero CPU utilization reported by a compute server).

Metadata such as sequential dependencies can be used to summarize the differences between consecutive timestamps or sequence numbers within a time series (or individual fragments of it) [Golab et al., 2009]. Furthermore, for spatiotemporal data, it is useful to identify the spatial distribution of locations or trajectories contained in the time series. (Of course, to compute statistics about trajectories such as their spatial distributions or length distributions, we must first extract trajectories from the data.)

Advanced techniques for time series profiling overlap with those for time series data mining. For a single time series, example techniques include detecting seasonality and frequent patterns (e.g., in a stock price time series, any period in which the price rises for several consecutive hours may be followed by a period in which the price drops for a few hours). For multiple time series analysis, it is useful to identify which time series are similar, which can be done through clustering or nearest-neighbor search.

In practice, time series data are typically collected incrementally over time, which emphasizes the need for incremental profiling. It is not feasible to re-profile an entire time series whenever a new datapoint arrives. We will revisit the important issue of incremental profiling (of relational and other types of data) in Chapter 9.

## 7.4  GRAPHS

A graph is composed of a set of vertices (nodes) and edges that connect pairs of vertices. Edges can be directed or undirected, and both edges and vertices may be weighted and/or labeled. Graphs naturally express relationships such as link relationships in the World Wide Web, friend and follower relationships in social media, or foreign key relationships in relational schemata.

Simple statistical properties of a graph include the *number of vertices, edges*, and *distinct labels*, the graph's *density* (the number of edges divided by the maximum possible number of edges where every vertex is directly connected to every other vertex), its *degree distribution* (where the degree of a vertex is the number of edges incident on it), and its *connectivity* (is the graph fully connected or does it consist of some number of disjoint components?). These statistics give an indication of the size of the graph and how well connected it is (including whether some vertices are more connected than others through the degree distribution). This is important for data analysts wishing to explore a new graph dataset and for graph data management systems, where connectivity and density metadata can help determine the best storage layout for the data.

Further statistical measures include the distribution of lengths of *shortest paths* between pairs of vertices and a characterization of *dense components* (e.g., how many cliques of different sizes are there?). It is also possible to identify *frequently occurring patterns* in a graph, e.g., "chains" or "stars."

There is also recent work on *keys* [Fan et al., 2015] and *functional dependencies* for graphs [Fan et al., 2016], which refer to entities represented by the vertices. For keys, the idea is to identify entities modeled by a graph by attribute value bindings and structural (topological) constraints. For example, suppose we have a graph database with music albums, where vertices correspond to albums and artists. An album can be uniquely identified by its title and by the artist's name (multiple artists may have released albums with the same name). Thus, a key for an album corresponds to a graph pattern with an album vertex (labeled with the album title), an artist vertex (labeled with the artist's name), and an edge connecting them. Similarly, the proposed FDs for graphs specify attribute dependencies as well as any associated withpological constraints. Discovering such FDs over graphs has recently been studied in Fan et al. [2018].

As was the case with time series data, real graphs are dynamic, e.g., in social networks, users join and leave, and friend or follower relationships are created or removed over time. Thus, graph profiling tools should be incremental to avoid re-profiling large graphs whenever vertices or edges are added or removed.

## 7.5 TEXT

Text profiling methods typically apply standard text analysis techniques to parse and annotate the data before generating metadata. These techniques include information extraction [Sarawagi, 2008], part-of-speech tagging [Brill, 1995], and text categorization [Keim and Oelke, 2007]. Text profiling tools can target individual documents, such as an article or a book, or sets (corpora) of documents, such as web pages, news articles, books, product reviews, or user comments.

Useful metadata that can be generated from pre-processed text can be classified into statistical and vocabulary measures. Statistical measures include distributions of parts of speech (what is the fraction of nouns, verbs, etc.?), paragraph lengths, sentence lengths, and word lengths (in terms of the number characters or syllables) [Holmes, 1994]. Vocabulary measures involve linguistic information and aim to measure style and diversity. These include frequencies of specific words, distinctiveness of the text (frequencies of words rarely occurring in the language, words which occur only once or twice in the given document, etc.), type-token ratio (the number of distinct words in a document divided by the total number of words), and Simpson's index (which quantifies the richness of the vocabulary).

Advanced text profiling techniques apply further processing and labeling such as sentiment/opinion mining [Liu, 2010, Pang and Lee, 2008] and topic modeling. Thus, the profiling output may include topics mentioned in the document and the polarity of any opinions expressed in the document (along with the topic about which the opinion is expressed). These statistics should be interpreted as approximate as even the state-of-the-art topic modeling and sentiment mining are not perfectly accurate due to the complexity of natural language.

As with other types of data, text profiling can be used to explore and learn about new datasets. Additionally, another interesting use case of text profiling is author attribution: predicting who wrote a piece of text based on various statistical or linguistic properties of the text [Holmes, 1994].

CHAPTER 8

# Data Profiling Tools

In this section, we discuss data profiling tools, how profiling results are visualized, and how users can interact with profiling components. We survey prototypes from research and industry that use profiling algorithms, and we address visualization and interaction when applicable.

## 8.1   RESEARCH PROTOTYPES

Table 8.1 lists recent data profiling tools from the literature. Aside from recent systems such as Metanome [Papenbrock et al., 2015a] and ProLOD++ [Abedjan et al., 2014a], data profiling is a supporting component of tools with a different primary purpose, such as data discovery, data cleaning, or data analytics.

Metanome is an open framework for running various profiling algorithms. It handles profiling algorithms and the datasets as external resources, which is why there are no profiling algorithms contained in the tool itself. Instead, researchers can add their own algorithms. However, Metanome includes popular dependency discovery algorithms such as DUCC [Heise et al., 2013], TANE [Huhtala et al., 1999], and BINDER [Papenbrock et al., 2015d].

ProLOD++ is a profiling framework with integrated profiling functionalities for exploring open RDF datasets [Abedjan et al., 2014a]. Profiling is particularly interesting in this setting as often times open RDF datasets lack the meta-information necessary to understand their structure and content.

As discussed in Section 6, profiling is useful in data cleaning and ETL. For example, the Bellman [Dasu et al., 2002] data quality browser displays column statistics (the number of rows, distinct values, and NULL values, the most frequently occurring values, etc.), and detects candidate keys with up to four columns. Bellman additionally offers a column similarity functionality that finds columns whose value or n-gram distributions are similar. This is helpful for discovering potential foreign keys and join paths. Another related application of Bellman was to profile the evolution of a database using value distributions and correlations [Dasu et al., 2006], answering question such as "Which tables change over time and in what ways (insertions, deletions, modifications), and which groups of tables tend to change in the same way?"

Potter's Wheel [Raman and Hellerstein, 2001] also supports column analysis, in particular detecting data types and syntactic structures/patterns. Its successor, Data Wrangler, provides the same functionalities [Kandel et al., 2011].

Recently, the Data Civilizer project introduced an end-to-end data integration framework with a data discovery component [Deng et al., 2017, Fernandez et al., 2016]. It embeds various

Table 8.1: Research tools with data profiling capabilities

| Tool | Main Goal | Profiling Capabilities |
|------|-----------|------------------------|
| Metanome [Papenbrock et al., 2015a] | Data Profiling | Columns statistics, rule discovery |
| ProLOD++ [Abedjan et al., 2014a] | LOD profiling and mining | General statistics, pattern discovery, unique discovery |
| Bellman [Dasu et al., 2002] | Data quality browser | Column statistics, column similarity, candidate key discovery |
| Potter's Wheel [Raman and Hellerstein, 2001] | Data quality, ETL | Column statistics (including value patterns) |
| Civilizer [Deng et al., 2017; Fernandez et al., 2016] | Data discovery | Column similarity |
| Data Auditor [Golab et al., 2010] | Rule discovery | CFD and CIND discovery |
| RuleMiner [Chu et al., 2014] | Rule discovery | Denial constraint discovery |
| MADLib [Hellerstein et al., 2012] | Machine learning | Simple column statistics |

profiling techniques such as IND discovery and column similarity in order to identify related tables.

A notable area of data cleaning that has a strong overlap with data profiling is rule-based data cleaning. Classical dependencies, such as FDs and INDs, as well as their conditional extensions, may be used to express the intended data semantics, and dependency violations may indicate possible data quality problems. Typically, users supply these data quality rules and dependencies, and systems such as GDR [Yakout et al., 2010], Nadeef [Dallachiesa et al., 2013a], Semandaq [Fan et al., 2008a], and StreamClean [Khoussainova et al., 2006] utilize them for data cleaning. Hence, these systems consume profiling results without performing the profiling itself; instead, they focus on languages for specifying rules and generating repairs. Since data quality rules are not always known apriori in unfamiliar and undocumented datasets, data profiling, and dependency discovery are important pre-requisites to data cleaning.

Within the context of data cleaning, there are two research prototype systems that perform rule discovery to some degree: Data Auditor [Golab et al., 2010] and RuleMiner [Chu et al.,

2014]. Data Auditor requires an FD as input and generates corresponding CFDs from the data. Additionally, Data Auditor considers FDs similar to the one that is provided by the user and generates corresponding CFDs. The idea is to see if a slightly modified FD can generate a more suitable CFD for the given relation instance. RuleMiner is designed to generate all reasonable FDs from a given dataset. RuleMiner expresses the discovered rules as *denial constraints*, which are universally quantified first-order logic formulas that subsume FDs, CFDs, INDs, and many others (see Section 5.4.1). Additionally, it provides a ranking functionality that discards trivial and subsumed rules, and ranks the discovered dependencies based on an *interestingness* score.

Finally, data profiling functionalities are also included in various data analytics frameworks. For example, the MADLib toolkit [Hellerstein et al., 2012] for scalable in-database analytics includes column statistics, such as count, count distinct, minimum and maximum values, quantiles, and the $k$ most frequently occurring values.

## 8.2   COMMERCIAL TOOLS

Data profiling algorithms are substantial components of any RDBMs. However, RDBMSs do not readily expose those metadata, the metadata are not always up-to-date and sometimes based only on samples, and their scope is usually limited to simple counts and cardinalities. More sophisticated approaches for cardinality estimation based on column dependencies have been proposed [Ilyas et al., 2004], but were not adopted mostly due to the trade-off between system complexity and practical gain. In typical scenarios, simple statistics over samples proved to be sufficient. This phenomenon can also be seen in other data management tools, such as tools for data integration and data analytics.

Table 8.2 lists examples of commercial tools with profiling functionalities, together with their capabilities and application focus, based on the respective product documentation. It is beyond the scope of this book to provide a market overview or compile feature matrices. A recent report by Gartner provides a comprehensive list of vendors and their data preparation tools that include data profiling algorithms for data cleansing and data preparation [Zaidi et al., 2017].

Similar to research prototypes, data profiling methods are usually embedded within commercial data preparation tools, which use the discovered frequent patterns and dependencies for data cleaning. Similarly, most Extract-Transform-Load tools have some profiling capabilities.

ETL and data cleaning tools include profiling algorithms that either run in the background and support the user in their decision making or can be used as explicit routines. For example, tools such as Tamr and Trifacta automatically generate various statistics and metadata, based on which the user can decide on suitable transformations or duplicate detection strategies. Classic ETL tools, such as Pentahoo or KNIME, include profiling functionalities such as aggregation, rule discovery and rule verification.

Data analytics platforms such as Tableau Desktop typically provide profiling functionality for aggregating values, creating histograms, identifying patterns, etc. An important aspect

Table 8.2: Commercial data profiling tools/components with their capabilities and application areas

| Vendor and Product | Features → Focus |
|---|---|
| **Attacama** DQ Analyzer | Statistics, patterns, uniques → Data exploration, ETL |
| **IBM** InfoSphere Information Analyzer | Statistics, patterns, multi-column dependencies → Data exchange, integration, cleansing |
| **Informatica** Data Quality | Structure, completeness, anomalies, dependencies → Business rules, cleansing |
| **Microsoft** SQL Server Data Profiling Task | Statistics, patterns, dependencies → ETL, cleansing |
| **Oracle** Enterprise Data Quality | Statistics, patterns, multi-column dependencies, text proling → Quality assessment, business rules, cleansing |
| **Paxata** Adaptive Data Preparation | Statistics, histograms, semantic data types → Exploration, cleansing, sharing |
| **SAP** Information Steward | Statistics, patterns, semantic data types, dependencies → ETL, modeling, cleansing |
| **Splunk** Enterprise / Hunk | Patterns, data mining → Search, analytics, visualization |
| **Talend** Data Profiles | Statistics, patterns, dependencies → ETL, cleansing |
| **Trifacta** | Statistics, patterns → Quality assessment, data transformation |
| **OpenRefne** | Statistics, patterns → Quality assessment, data transformation |
| **Tamr** | Statistics, uniques, cardinalities → Schema matching, duplicate detection |
| **KNIME** | Statistics, patterns, rules → Quality assessment, data transformation |
| **Pentahoo** | Statistics, patterns, rules → Quality assessment, data transformation |
| **Tablaeu products** | Statistics, patterns, histograms → data analytics and business intelligence |

of these kinds of tools is their usability and visualization capabilities. Typically aimed at less technical staff, these products have to provide interactive visualizations that expose interesting characteristics about the data.

CHAPTER 9

# Data Profiling Challenges

Chapter 7 examined data profiling for new types of data, introducing new challenges. Here, we return to relational data, but most of the challenges we identify below are equally true for other types of data. While research and industry have made significant advances in developing efficient and often scalable methods, the focus of data profiling has been a quite static and stand-alone use case: given a dataset, discover a well defined set of metadata. Many open challenges remain. They include both functional challenges, such as keeping the metadata up-to-date despite changes to the data, and non-functional challenges, such as better scalability, distribution and benchmarking. We explore these and others in this chapter.

## 9.1 FUNCTIONAL CHALLENGES

Functional challenges extend data profiling capabilities. They address new requirements that may arise from the nature of the data to be profiled and from new ways of interacting with data profiling systems and their results.

### 9.1.1 PROFILING DYNAMIC DATA

Data profiling describes a fixed instance of a dataset at a particular time. Since many applications work on frequently changing, dynamic data, it is desirable to re-examine a dataset after a change, such as a deletion, insertion, or update, in order to obtain up-to-date metadata. Data profiling methods should be able to efficiently handle such moving targets, in particular without re-profiling the entire dataset with one of the algorithms described so far. For individual columns, simple aggregates are easy to maintain incrementally, but many statistics needed for column analysis, such as distinct value counts, cannot be maintained exactly using limited space and time. For these aggregates, stream-sketching techniques [Ganguly, 2007] may be used to maintain approximate answers. There are also techniques for continuously updating discovered association rules [Tsai et al., 1999] and clusters [Ester et al., 1998].

Existing approaches for dependency discovery may be too time-consuming for repeated execution on the entire dataset. Thus, it is necessary to incrementally update the results without processing the complete dataset again. One example is Swan, an approach for unique discovery on dynamic datasets with insertions and deletions [Abedjan et al., 2014b] as reported in Section 4.3.5. The intuition is to maintain carefully selected indexes for "vulnerable" columns, i.e., columns where a few changes can have an effect on the set of UCCs. Also, Wang et al. present an approach for maintaining discovered FDs after data deletions [Wang et al., 2003]. From a data cleaning standpoint, there are solutions for incremental detection of FD and CFD violations [Fan et al., 2012], and incremental data repairing with respect to FDs and CFDs [Cong et al., 2007]. However, in general, incremental solutions for FDs, CFDs, INDs, and CINDs on growing and changing datasets remain challenges for future research.

Incremental profiling typically assumes periodic updates or periodic profiling runs. A further use case is to update profiling results while (transactional) data are created or updated, i.e., perform *continuous profiling*. If the profiling results can be expressed as a query, and if they are to be performed only on a temporal window of the data, this use case can be served by data stream management systems [Golab and Özsu, 2010]. If this is not the case, continuous profiling methods need to be developed, whose results can be displayed in a dashboard. It is particularly important to find a good tradeoff between recency, accuracy, and resource consumption. Use cases for continuous profiling include internet traffic monitoring or the profiling of incoming search queries.

## 9.1.2   INTERACTIVE PROFILING

In many use cases, data profiling is an inherently user-oriented task or a task typically invoked manually by a user. Often, the produced metadata is consumed directly by the user or it is at least viewed by a user before being put to use in some application, such as schema design or data cleansing. Involving the user during the algorithmic part of data profiling, namely "interactive profiling" is an unaddressed challenge. We describe two forms of such interactive profiling. The first, online profiling, allows users to interact with profiling results while they are created. The second challenge is to allow users an efficient back and forth between profiling and cleansing the data.

**Online profiling**   Despite the optimization efforts described in this book, a data profiling run might last longer than a user is willing to wait in front of a screen with nothing to look at. Online profiling presents intermediate results as they are created. However, simply hooking the graphical interface into existing algorithms is usually not sufficient: data that is sorted by some attribute or has a skewed order yields misleading intermediate results. Solutions might be approximate or sampling-based methods, whose results gracefully improve as more computation is invested. Naturally, such intermediate results do not reflect the properties of the entire dataset. Thus, some form of confidence, along with a progress indicator, can be shown to allow an early interpretation of the results. Apart from entertaining users during computation, an advantage of online profiling is that the user may abort the profiling run altogether. For instance, a user might decide early on that the dataset is not interesting (or clean) enough for the task at hand.

Another solution is to design *progressive* profiling algorithms, which optimize toward producing as many results as possible as early as possible, similar to progressive deduplication [Altowim et al., 2014, Papenbrock et al., 2015c, Whang et al., 2013]. If progressive profiling could be combined with pruning strategies that filter for usefulness/genuineness of the profiling results (see Section 9.1.4), the entire profiling result might never need to be generated.

**Profiling of queries and views**    In many cases, data profiling is done to clean the data or the schema to some extent, for instance, to be able to insert it into a data warehouse or to integrate it with some other dataset. However, each cleansing step changes the data, and thus implicitly also the metadata produced by profiling. In general, after each cleansing step, a new profiling run should be performed. For instance, only after cleaning up zip-code does the functional dependency with city become apparent. Or only after deduplication does the uniqueness of email addresses reveal itself.

Future profiling systems might allow users to virtually interact with the data and re-compute profiling results after each interaction. For instance, the profiling system might show a 96% uniqueness for a certain column. The user might recognize that the attribute should be completely unique and is in fact a key. Without performing the actual cleansing, a user might want to virtually declare the column to be a key and re-perform profiling on this virtually cleansed data. Only then a foreign key for this attribute might be recognized.

A key enabling technology for this kind of interaction is the ability to efficiently re-perform profiling on slightly changed data, as discussed in Section 9.1.1. In the same manner, profiling results can be efficiently achieved on query results: while calculating the query result, profiling results can be generated on the side, thus showing a user not only the result itself, but also the nature of that data.

**Data cleansing**    One of the major use cases for data profiling is data cleansing. Since data cleansing requires expert feedback, profiling methods to support it must be interactive. Recently, several approaches have emerged to support this combination. For instance, Thirumuruganathan et al. [2017] present an approach in which experts can validate FDs or data errors. The system helps to optimize the number of decisions the user needs to make. After each decision, the set of FDs and supposed data errors is updated before presenting the next candidates for validation. With the Falcon system, He et al. [2016] present a method to help users iteratively create a set of update queries to clean the data using dependencies to discover attributes with a high update-correlation. A comprehensive summary of data profiling techniques and their combination with data cleansing is in the recent book by Chu and Ilyas [2019].

For all of the above suggestions, new algorithms and data structures are needed to enhance the user experience of data profiling.

## 9.1.3    PROFILING FOR INTEGRATION

Data integration is an important use case of traditional data profiling methods. Knowledge about the properties of different data sources is important to create correct schema mappings and data transformations, and to correctly standardize and cleanse the data. For instance, knowledge of inclusion dependencies might suggest ways to join two unrelated tables [Fernandez et al., 2018].

Data profiling can reach beyond such supportive tasks and assess the *integrability* or ease of integration of datasets, and thus also indicate the necessary integration effort, which is vital to project planning. Integration effort might be expressed in terms of similarity, but also in terms of man-months or in terms of which tools are needed.

Like integration projects themselves, integrability has two dimensions, namely schematic fit and data fit. *Structural fit* is the degree to which two schemata complement and overlap each other and can be determined using schema matching techniques [Euzenat and Shvaiko, 2013]. Smith et al. [2009] have recognized that schema matching techniques often play the role of profiling tools. rather than using them to derive schema mappings and perform data transformation, they might assess project feasibility. Finally, the mere matching of schema elements might not suffice as a profiling-for-integration result; additional column metadata can provide further details about the integration difficulty.

*Data fit* is the (estimated) number of real-world objects that are represented in both datasets, or that are represented multiple times in a single dataset and how different they are. Such multiple representations are typically identified using entity matching methods (also known as record linkage, entity resolution, duplicate detection, etc.) [Christen, 2012]. Kruse et al. [2015b] combine these two dimensions into a common estimation framework as a first attempt to explicitly perform data profiling with the goal of integration.

## 9.1.4 INTERPRETING PROFILING RESULTS

As we have observed in the previous chapters, the results of data profiling can be very large. For instance, the number of functional dependencies in typical real-world datasets can reach into the hundreds of thousands or even millions [Papenbrock and Naumann, 2016]. Clearly, most of such dependencies are spurious: they happen to be true for the dataset at hand but have no useful meaning. Of course, these dependencies are still useful, for instance during query optimization. However, the ability to handle large result sets and to interpret them is needed. Research in this area is just beginning and we highlight a few results.

**Managing and mining profiling results**   Metadata management is a traditional research area, which is usually concerned with managing schemata, basic statistics and their evolution. Storing vast quantities of dependencies is a more difficult undertaking. While there are several tools and approaches that incorporate data profiles for specific data management scenarios (e.g., Andritsos et al. [2002], Dasu et al. [2002], and Deng et al. [2017]), none of them offers a general solution for metadata management. As explained in Kruse et al. [2017a], a general system needs to handle not only the large volumes, but also the variety of metadata (as well exemplified in this book) and finally needs to be able to integrate them into a common picture about a given dataset.

The Metacrate system is specifically designed to ingest large data profiling results, query them, and analyze them with a Scala-based data flow API, and finally visualize the results with some initial visualization schemes [Kruse et al., 2017a]. Two visualization examples are shown in Figure 9.1.

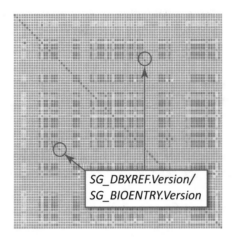

Figure 9.1: Attribute similarity matrix (left) and sunburst chart with the highlighted FD Title, Authors, Location → CRC (right) from Kruse et al. [2017a].

**Visualizing profiling results** Visualizing profiling results is of utmost importance due to their large quantity, their intrinsic complexity, and the need to carefully interpret them, as many results are spurious. A concrete suggestion for a visual data profiling tool is the Profiler system by Kandel et al. [2012], which aims at data cleansing scenarios and targets only simple type of metadata, such as value distributions and other aggregations. That work was ultimately included in the Trifacta product.

In general, a strong cooperation between the database community, which produces the data and metadata to be visualized, and the visualization community, which enables users to understand and make use of the data, is needed to advance the ability to interpret data profiling results for its various use cases.

**Genuineness of profiling results** In the previous paragraphs, we have hinted at the fact that many data profiling results, in particular dependencies, are spurious, giving rise to the problem of (automatically) identifying *genuine* dependencies, i.e., those that have a real-world meaning and should hold not only for the instance at hand but for all instances of the particular schema. That is, dependency detection algorithms find all syntactically valid dependencies, but not all of them are semantically valid.

Research on classifying dependencies as genuine or non-genuine is in its early stages. For inclusion dependencies, two works have successfully attempted to classify them as foreign keys or as spurious. Rostin et al. propose a set of features and use a decision-tree method for the classification [Rostin et al., 2009]. The ten features include measures that count how many dependent and referenced values exist, the similarity of columns names, and the overall graph of inclusion dependencies within the database at hand. Zhang et al. assume that the data of a foreign key should well represent a sample from the key column it references, and introduce a "randomness" metric to discover both single-column and multi-column foreign keys [Zhang et al., 2010].

Understanding the genuineness of keys and functional dependencies is an open challenge. Papenbrock et al. propose a first solution in the context of automatic normalization of tables [Papenbrock and Naumann, 2017b]. To automatically decompose/normalize a given table, we must decide which unique columns combinations are indeed keys and which functional dependency might be violating the normal form. The authors suggest simple, yet effective features, such as the number of involved attributes, their position in the schema, and the number of repeated values.

A different approach to gauge the genuineness of a functional dependency is to determine its probability. For instance, given two arbitrarily chosen tuples, the $pdep(X, Y)$ measure is defined as the probability that the tuples agree on $Y$ given that they agree on $X$ [Piatetsky-Shapiro and Matheus, 1993]. That is, the measure gives the expected probability for correctly guessing $r[Y]$ for a randomly selected record $R$ by selecting a $Y$-value based on the conditional probability distribution of $Y$ given $r[X]$. Such measures can serve as a basis to rank FDs for genuineness.

Finally, recent work by Berti-Equille et al. [2018] proposes a different interpretation of genuineness of functional dependencies. The authors predict which FDs are in fact valid on a clean and complete dataset, even when discovery algorithms can read only a dirty version of the dataset with missing values. To achieve this, they introduced and tested several variations of a genuineness score based on probabilistic imputation and the likelihood of the FD to be correct. Given a score for each discovered FD, the top-k% are considered to be genuine.

## 9.2  NON-FUNCTIONAL CHALLENGES

Apart from obvious non-functional challenges, such as improving runtime efficiency and memory consumption, which are the main focus of most of the methods described in this book, some new challenges arise, including profiling on modern data processing architectures and systematically assessing profiling approaches.

### 9.2.1  EFFICIENCY AND SCALABILITY

While research has made significant steps in the past decade to handle large datasets, the exponential complexity of many data profiling problems is irrefutable and can be observed in runtime results of research papers. One way to solve profiling problems on larger datasets is to employ parallel and distributed algorithms. Another approach to improve efficiency and thus usefulness of data profiling on datasets with many records is to allow approximate results, thus not reading all data and not comparing all pairs of records. To deal with datasets with very many columns, one can restrict the size of the dependencies to be detected, so that the exponential number of combinations is avoided. For instance, limiting UCC discovery to UCCs of size five might be reasonable when the application is to find candidate keys. Finally, measures to assess the quality or genuineness of a dependencies might be used to guide pruning of the search space and thus speed up detection algorithms.

In summary, the efficiency and scalability of data profiling methods are not yet at a point where *any* dataset can be analyzed without performance concerns. As datasets grow, throwing iron at the exponential problem has its limits and smart algorithms and data structures form a more promising avenue of research and development.

## 9.2.2   PROFILING ON NEW ARCHITECTURES

Data management on modern hardware and on novel software architectures is a hot topic with much potential to push the envelope of traditional data management tasks. Many new systems make use of modern hardware, such as GPUs, FPGAs, NUMA architectures, and compute clusters. And emerging software architectures, such as column-oriented data storage, soft-schema databases, and vector processing, are being adopted.

The overarching research question is how to make use of or adapt these new systems to improve the efficiency of data profiling methods. For instance, column-store systems appear to have a natural computational advantage, at least in terms of the column analysis tasks we discussed in Chapter 3, since they can directly fetch the column of interest and compute statistics on it. However, if all columns are to be profiled, the entire dataset must be read and the only remaining advantage of column stores may be their potential compression.

Further challenges arise when performing data profiling on key-value stores: typically, the values contain some structured data, without any enforced schemata. Thus, even defining expected results on such "soft schema" values is a challenge, and a first step must involve schema discovery.

## 9.2.3   BENCHMARKING PROFILING METHODS

To systematically evaluate different methods and architectures for data profiling, a corresponding *data profiling benchmark* is needed. It should include (i) a set of profiling *tasks*, (ii) realistic *data* on which the tasks shall be executed, and (iii) *measures* to evaluate efficiency. For (i), the classification of profiling tasks in Figure 2.1 (see Page 8) can serve as a guide. Arguably, the most difficult part of establishing a benchmark is to (ii) provide a set of real-world datasets that covers a wide range of metadata properties, such as datasets with many and with few rows, with many and with few columns, with different uniquenesses of columns and different value distributions, with large and with small UCCs, with many and with few FDs of specific sizes, etc.

Lacking such a variety of datasets, one could generate such data. However, it is not trivial to create a valid database instance given, e.g., a fixed set of FD-sizes. Consider a dataset specification demanding 10 columns, and exactly five minimal FDs of size 1, six FDs of size 3, and four FDs of size 7. Creating such a dataset must solve two tasks. First, the position of each FD in the lattice of column combinations must be decided. Placing one FD can have implications on the placement of the remaining FDs, which may no longer minimal, etc. Then, one must create data to precisely match the fixed set of dependencies, in essence creating an Armstrong table [Hartmann et al., 2015]. In addition, if some errors, i.e., violations of constraints, are to be inserted, or if conditional dependencies are needed, the task becomes even more daunting.

Finally, the measures for (iii) need to be carefully selected. In practice, data profiling algorithms often fail due to memory consumption rather than exceed certain runtimes. Thus, both computational complexity and space complexity are relevant. Space complexity can be refined further to consider whether an algorithm is able to effectively spill to disk and thus scale to large search spaces. In addition to these traditional measures, evaluation of approximate results should be included.

CHAPTER 10

# Conclusions

In this book, we provided a conceptual and technical overview of data profiling: the set of activities and processes for extracting metadata, statistics, and dependencies from a given dataset or database. We started with a discussion of simple single-column profiling, such as detecting data types, summarizing value distributions, and identifying frequently occurring patterns. We then discussed multi-column profiling, with an emphasis on algorithms for discovering unique column combinations, functional dependencies among columns, and inclusion dependencies among tables. While the focus of this book is on exact profiling of relational data, we provided a brief discussion of approximate profiling using data sketches and profiling non-relational data, such as text and graphs.

As the amount of data and the number of individuals working with data increase, data profiling will continue to be an important data management problem in research and practice. Additionally, as we discussed in Chapter 9, recent trends in data management have introduced new challenges to effective data profiling and have amplified traditional challenges arising from the very large search space and solution space. To address these challenges, we expect to see new research in the near future along the following two lines.

1. Technical innovations, including new data profiling algorithms that can scale to very large datasets and exploit modern hardware trends such as distributed computing; incremental data profiling algorithms that can handle insertions, deletions, and updates without re-profiling all the data; and new algorithms for profiling non-relational data such as text, graphs, and data streams.

2. User-oriented innovations to help users visualize, prioritize, interpret, and make effective use of data profiling results.

We close with a reminder of the limitations of data profiling methods. A significant limitation is that data profiling is performed on a snapshot of the data at a particular time, meaning that the collected statistics may change over time. While incremental profiling techniques exist for some tasks (recall Section 9.1.1), data profiling tools are not designed to predict future data. Furthermore, manual intervention may be required to check whether the results of data profiling are semantically meaningful (e.g., to check which of the reported unique column combinations are potential keys).

# Bibliography

Ziawasch Abedjan and Felix Naumann. Advancing the discovery of unique column combinations. In *Proc. of the International Conference on Information and Knowledge Management (CIKM)*, pages 1565–1570, 2011. DOI: 10.1145/2063576.2063801 22, 31, 34, 35

Ziawasch Abedjan and Felix Naumann. Synonym analysis for predicate expansion. In *Proc. of the Extended Semantic Web Conference (ESWC)*, pages 140–154, Montpellier, France, 2013. DOI: 10.1007/978-3-642-38288-8_10 94

Ziawasch Abedjan, Johannes Lorey, and Felix Naumann. Reconciling ontologies and the Web of data. In *Proc. of the International Conference on Information and Knowledge Management (CIKM)*, pages 1532–1536, 2012. DOI: 10.1145/2396761.2398467 94

Ziawasch Abedjan, Toni Grütze, Anja Jentzsch, and Felix Naumann. Profiling and mining RDF data with ProLOD++. In *Proc. of the International Conference on Data Engineering (ICDE)*, 2014a. DOI: 10.1109/icde.2014.6816740 94, 97

Ziawasch Abedjan, Jorge-Arnulfo Quiané-Ruiz, and Felix Naumann. Detecting unique column combinations on dynamic data. In *Proc. of the International Conference on Data Engineering (ICDE)*, pages 1036–1047, 2014b. DOI: 10.1109/icde.2014.6816721 31, 38, 103

Ziawasch Abedjan, Patrick Schulze, and Felix Naumann. DFD: Efficient functional dependency discovery. In *Proc. of the International Conference on Information and Knowledge Management (CIKM)*, pages 949–958, 2014c. DOI: 10.1145/2661829.2661884 31, 39, 45

Ziawasch Abedjan, Cuneyt G. Akcora, Mourad Ouzzani, Paolo Papotti, and Michael Stonebraker. Temporal rules discovery for web data cleaning. *Proc. of the VLDB Endowment*, 9(4):336–347, December 2015a. DOI: 10.14778/2856318.2856328 81

Ziawasch Abedjan, Lukasz Golab, and Felix Naumann. Profiling relational data: A survey. *VLDB Journal*, 24(4):557–581, 2015b. DOI: 10.1007/s00778-015-0389-y xv, 22, 76

Ziawasch Abedjan, Lukasz Golab, and Felix Naumann. Data profiling. In *Proc. of the International Conference on Data Engineering (ICDE)*, pages 1432–1435, 2016. DOI: 10.1109/icde.2016.7498363 xv

Ziawasch Abedjan, Lukasz Golab, and Felix Naumann. Data profiling. In *Proc. of the International Conference on Management of Data (SIGMOD)*, pages 1747–1751, 2017. DOI: 10.1109/icde.2016.7498363 xv

Divyakant Agrawal, Philip Bernstein, Elisa Bertino, Susan Davidson, Umeshwar Dayal, Michael Franklin, Johannes Gehrke, Laura Haas, Alon Halevy, Jiawei Han, H. V. Jagadish, Alexandros Labrinidis, Sam Madden, Yannis Papakonstantinou, Jignesh M. Patel, Raghu Ramakrishnan, Kenneth Ross, Cyrus Shahabi, Dan Suciu, Shiv Vaithyanathan, and Jennifer Widom. Challenges and opportunities with Big Data. *Technical Report*, Computing Community Consortium, `http://cra.org/ccc/docs/init/bigdatawhitepaper.pdf`, 2012. DOI: 10.14778/2367502.2367572 1

Rakesh Agrawal and Ramakrishnan Srikant. Fast algorithms for mining association rules in large databases. In *Proc. of the International Conference on Very Large Databases (VLDB)*, pages 487–499, 1994. 34, 39, 41, 69

Yasser Altowim, Dmitri V. Kalashnikov, and Sharad Mehrotra. Progressive approach to relational entity resolution. *Proc. of the VLDB Endowment*, 7(11):999–1010, 2014. DOI: 10.14778/2732967.2732975 104

Martin Andersson. *Extracting an Entity Relationship Schema from a Relational Database Through Reverse Engineering*, pages 403–419, Springer, Heidelberg, 1994. DOI: 10.1007/3-540-58786-1_93 88

Periklis Andritsos, Ronald Fagin, Ariel Fuxman, Laura M. Haas, Mauricio A. Hernández, C. T. Howard Ho, Anastasios Kementsietsidis, Renée J. Miller, Felix Naumann, Lucian Popa, Yannis Velegrakis, Charlotte Vilarem, and Ling-Ling Yan. Schema management. *IEEE Data Engineering Bulletin*, 25(3):32–38, 2002. 106

Periklis Andritsos, Renée J. Miller, and Panayiotis Tsaparas. Information-theoretic tools for mining database structure from large data sets. In *Proc. of the International Conference on Management of Data (SIGMOD)*, pages 731–742, 2004. DOI: 10.1145/1007568.1007650 89

Marcelo Arenas, Jonny Daenen, Frank Neven, Martin Ugarte, Jan Van den Bussche, and Stijn Vansummeren. Discovering XSD keys from XML data. In *Proc. of the International Conference on Management of Data (SIGMOD)*, pages 61–72, 2013. DOI: 10.1145/2463676.2463705 93

William W. Armstrong. Dependency structures of database relationships. *Information Processing*, 74(1):580–583, 1974. 21

Morton M. Astrahan, Mario Schkolnick, and Whang Kyu-Young. Approximating the number of unique values of an attribute without sorting. *Information Systems (IS)*, 12(1):11–15, 1987. DOI: 10.1016/0306-4379(87)90014-7 17

Paolo Atzeni and Nicola M. Morfuni. Functional dependencies and constraints on null values in database relations. *Information and Control*, 70(1):1–31, 1986. DOI: 10.1016/s0019-9958(86)80022-5 30

Sören Auer, Jan Demter, Michael Martin, and Jens Lehmann.   LODStats—An extensible framework for high-performance dataset analytics.   In *Proc. of the International Conference on Knowledge Engineering and Knowledge Management (EKAW)*, pages 353–362, 2012. DOI: 10.1007/978-3-642-33876-2_31 94

Jaume Baixeries. Computing similarity dependencies with pattern structures. In *International Conference on Concept Lattice Applications (CLA)*, pages 175–186, 2012. 78

Sridevi Baskaran, Alexander Keller, Fei Chiang, Lukasz Golab, and Jaroslaw Szlichta.   Efficient discovery of ontology functional dependencies.   In *Proc. of the International Conference on Information and Knowledge Management (CIKM)*, pages 1847–1856, 2017. DOI: 10.1145/3132847.3132879 80

Renaud Bassée and Jef Wijsen.   Neighborhood dependencies for prediction.   In *Proc. of the Pacific-Asia Conference on Knowledge Discovery and Data Mining (PAKDD)*, pages 562–567, Springer Berlin Heidelberg, 2001. DOI: 10.1007/3-540-45357-1_59 78

Jana Bauckmann, Ulf Leser, and Felix Naumann. Efficiently computing inclusion dependencies for schema discovery. In *ICDE Workshops*, page 2, 2006. DOI: 10.1109/icdew.2006.54 56, 64

Jana Bauckmann, Ulf Leser, Felix Naumann, and Veronique Tietz.   Efficiently detecting inclusion dependencies.   In *Proc. of the International Conference on Data Engineering (ICDE)*, pages 1448–1450, Istanbul, Turkey, 2007. DOI: 10.1109/icde.2007.369032 9

Catriel Beeri and Philip A. Bernstein. Computational problems related to the design of normal form relational schemas. *ACM Transactions on Database Systems (TODS)*, 4(1):30–59, 1979. DOI: 10.1145/320064.320066 21

Catriel Beeri, Ronald Fagin, and John H. Howard. A complete axiomatization for functional and multivalued dependencies in database relations. In *Proc. of the International Conference on Management of Data (SIGMOD)*, pages 47–61, 1977. DOI: 10.1145/509412.509414 86

Catriel Beeri, Martin Dowd, Ronald Fagin, and Richard Statman. On the structure of Armstrong relations for functional dependencies. *Journal of the ACM*, 31(1):30–46, 1984. DOI: 10.1145/2422.322414 29

Siegfried Bell and Peter Brockhausen. Discovery of data dependencies in relational databases. *Technical Report*, Universität Dortmund, 1995. 56, 60

Zohra Bellahsene, Angela Bonifati, and Erhard Rahm. *Schema Matching and Mapping*, 1st ed., Springer, Heidelberg, 2011. DOI: 10.1007/978-3-642-16518-4 91

Frank Benford. The law of anomalous numbers. *Proc. of the American Philosophical Society*, 78(4):551–572, 1938. 13

## 116 BIBLIOGRAPHY

Philip A. Bernstein. Synthesizing third normal form relations from functional dependencies. *ACM Transactions on Database Systems (TODS)*, 1(4):277–298, 1976. DOI: 10.1145/320493.320489 89

Laure Berti-Equille, Hazar Harmouch, Felix Naumann, and Noël Novelli. Discovery of genuine functional dependencies from relational data with missing values. *Proc. of the VLDB Endowment*, 11(8):880–892, 2018. DOI: 10.14778/3204028.3204032 108

Leopoldo E. Bertossi. *Database Repairing and Consistent Query Answering*. Morgan & Claypool Publishers, 2011. DOI: 10.2200/s00379ed1v01y201108dtm020 84

Geert Jan Bex, Frank Neven, and Stijn Vansummeren. Inferring XML schema definitions from XML data. In *Proc. of the International Conference on Very Large Databases (VLDB)*, pages 998–1009, 2007. 93

Garrett Birkhoff. *Lattice Theory*, 1st ed., American Mathematical Society, Providence, RI, 1940. DOI: 10.1090/coll/025 24

Thomas Bläsius, Tobias Friedrich, and Martin Schirneck. The parameterized complexity of dependency detection in relational databases. In *Proc. of the International Symposium on Parameterized and Exact Computation (IPEC)*, pages 6:1–6:13, 2017. DOI: 10.4230/LIPIcs.IPEC.2016.6 29

Tobias Bleifuß, Susanne Bülow, Johannes Frohnhofen, Julian Risch, Georg Wiese, Sebastian Kruse, Thorsten Papenbrock, and Felix Naumann. Approximate discovery of functional dependencies for large datasets. In *Proc. of the International Conference on Information and Knowledge Management (CIKM)*, pages 1803–1812, 2016. DOI: 10.1145/2983323.2983781 83

Tobias Bleifuß, Sebastian Kruse, and Felix Naumann. Efficient denial constraint discovery with hydra. *Proc. of the VLDB Endowment*, 11(3):311–323, 2017. DOI: 10.14778/3157794.3157800 84

Philip Bohannon, Wenfei Fan, and Floris Geerts. Conditional functional dependencies for data cleaning. In *Proc. of the International Conference on Data Engineering (ICDE)*, pages 746–755, 2007. DOI: 10.1109/icde.2007.367920 76, 89

Christoph Böhm, Johannes Lorey, and Felix Naumann. Creating voiD descriptions for web-scale data. *Journal of Web Semantics*, 9(3):339–345, 2011. DOI: 10.2139/ssrn.3199519 94

Patrick Bosc, Didier Dubois, and Henri Prade. Fuzzy functional dependencies—An overview and a critical discussion. In *Proc. of the International Fuzzy Systems Conference*, pages 325–330, 1994. DOI: 10.1109/fuzzy.1994.343753 78

Loreto Bravo, Wenfei Fan, and Shuai Ma. Extending dependencies with conditions. In *Proc. of the International Conference on Very Large Databases (VLDB)*, pages 243–254, 2007. 10, 76, 77

Eric Brill. Transformation-based error-driven learning and natural language processing: A case study in part-of-speech tagging. *Computational Linguistics*, 21(4):543–565, 1995. 96

Paul G. Brown and Peter J. Hass. BHUNT: Automatic discovery of fuzzy algebraic constraints in relational data. In *Proc. of the VLDB Endowment*, pages 668–679, 2003. 83

Peter Buneman, Susan B. Davidson, Wenfei Fan, Carmem S. Hara, and Wang Chiew Tan. Reasoning about keys for XML. *Information Systems (IS)*, 28(8):1037–1063, 2003. DOI: 10.1016/s0306-4379(03)00028-0 93

Loredana Caruccio, Vincenzo Deufemia, and Giuseppe Polese. Relaxed functional dependencies—A survey of approaches. *IEEE Transactions on Knowledge and Data Engineering (TKDE)*, 28(1):147–165, 2016. DOI: 10.1109/tkde.2015.2472010 10, 75, 76, 78, 83

Marco A. Casanova, Ronald Fagin, and Christos H. Papadimitriou. Inclusion dependencies and their interaction with functional dependencies. In *Proc. of the Symposium on Principles of Database Systems (PODS)*, pages 171–176, 1982. DOI: 10.1145/588140.588141 23

Marco A. Casanova, Luiz Tucherman, and Antonio L. Furtado. Enforcing inclusion dependencies and referential integrity. In *Proc. of the International Conference on Very Large Databases (VLDB)*, pages 38–49, 1988. 90

Aaron Ceglar and John F. Roddick. Association mining. *ACM Computing Surveys*, 38(2):1–42, 2006. DOI: 10.1145/1132956.1132958 4

Varun Chandola and Vipin Kumar. Summarization—Compressing data into an informative representation. *Knowledge and Information Systems (KAIS)*, 12(3):355–378, 2007. DOI: 10.1007/s10115-006-0039-1 16

Shi-Kuo K. Chang, Vincenzo Deufemia, Giuseppe Polese, and Mario Vacca. A normalization framework for multimedia databases. *IEEE Transactions on Knowledge and Data Engineering (TKDE)*, 19(12):1666–1679, 2007. DOI: 10.1109/tkde.2007.190651 78

Surajit Chaudhuri. An overview of query optimization in relational systems. In *Proc. of the Symposium on Principles of Database Systems (PODS)*, pages 34–43, 1998. DOI: 10.1145/275487.275492 90

Jianer Chen and Fenghui Zhang. On product covering in 3-tier supply chain models: Natural complete problems for w[3] and w[4]. *Theoretical Computer Science*, 363(3):278–288, 2006. DOI: 10.1007/11496199_43 30

Ming-syan Chen, Jiawei Hun, and Philip S. Yu. Data mining: An overview from a database perspective. *IEEE Transactions on Knowledge and Data Engineering (TKDE)*, 8:866–883, 1996. DOI: 10.1109/69.553155 4

Yang Chen, Sean Goldberg, Daisy Zhe Wang, and Soumitra Siddharth Johri. Ontological pathfinding. In *Proc. of the International Conference on Management of Data (SIGMOD)*, pages 835–846, New York, ACM, 2016. DOI: 10.1145/2882903.2882954 94

Fei Chiang and Renée J. Miller. Discovering data quality rules. *Proc. of the VLDB Endowment*, 1:1166–1177, 2008. DOI: 10.14778/1453856.1453980 77

Byron Choi. What are real DTDs like? In *Proc. of the ACM SIGMOD Workshop on the Web and Databases (WebDB)*, pages 43–48, 2002. 93

Peter Christen. *Data Matching*. Springer Verlag, Berlin Heidelberg, New York, 2012. DOI: 10.1007/978-3-642-31164-2 106

Xu Chu and Ihab Ilyas. *Data Cleaning*. Association for Computing Machinery, Morgan & Claypool, New York, 2019. DOI: 10.1145/2882903.2912574 105

Xu Chu, I. F. Ilyas, and P. Papotti. Holistic data cleaning: Putting violations into context. In *Proc. of the International Conference on Data Engineering (ICDE)*, pages 458–469, 2013a. DOI: 10.1109/icde.2013.6544847 90

Xu Chu, Ihab F. Ilyas, and Paolo Papotti. Discovering denial constraints. *Proc. of the VLDB Endowment*, 6(13):1498–1509, 2013b. DOI: 10.14778/2536258.2536262 84

Xu Chu, Ihab Ilyas, Paolo Papotti, and Yin Ye. RuleMiner: Data quality rules discovery. In *Proc. of the International Conference on Data Engineering (ICDE)*, pages 1222–1225, 2014. DOI: 10.1109/icde.2014.6816746 98

Edgar F. Codd. A relational model of data for large shared data banks. *Communications of the ACM*, 13(6):377–387, 1970. DOI: 10.1145/357980.358007 89

Edgar F. Codd. Further normalization of the data base relational model. *IBM Research Report*, San Jose, CA, 1971. 21

Gao Cong, Wenfei Fan, Floris Geerts, Xibei Jia, and Shuai Ma. Improving data quality: Consistency and accuracy. In *Proc. of the International Conference on Very Large Databases (VLDB)*, pages 315–326, 2007. 90, 104

Graham Cormode and S. Muthukrishnan. An improved data stream summary: The count-min sketch and its applications. *Journal of Algorithms*, 55(1):58–75, 2005. DOI: 10.1016/j.jalgor.2003.12.001 17

Graham Cormode, Flip Korn, S. Muthukrishnan, and Divesh Srivastava. Space- and time-efficient deterministic algorithms for biased quantiles over data streams. In *Proc. of the Symposium on Principles of Database Systems (PODS)*, pages 263–272, 2006. DOI: 10.1145/1142351.1142389 13

Graham Cormode, Lukasz Golab, Korn Flip, Andrew McGregor, Divesh Srivastava, and Xi Zhang. Estimating the confidence of conditional functional dependencies. In *Proc. of the International Conference on Management of Data (SIGMOD)*, pages 469–482, 2009. DOI: 10.1145/1559845.1559895 77

Graham Cormode, Minos N. Garofalakis, Peter J. Haas, and Chris Jermaine. Synopses for massive data: Samples, histograms, wavelets, sketches. *Foundations and Trends in Databases*, 4(1–3):1–294, 2011. DOI: 10.1561/1900000004 7, 10, 17, 83

Stavros S. Cosmadakis, Paris C. Kanellakis, and Nicolas Spyratos. Partition semantics for relations. *Journal of Computer and System Sciences*, 33(2):203–233, 1986. DOI: 10.1016/0022-0000(86)90019-x 28

Peter Crawley and Robert P. Dilworth. *Algebraic Theory of Lattices*, 1st ed., Prentice Hall, Englewood Cliffs, NJ, 1973. 24

Michele Dallachiesa, Amr Ebaid, Ahmed Eldawy, Ahmed Elmagarmid, Ihab F. Ilyas, Mourad Ouzzani, and Nan Tang. NADEEF: A commodity data cleaning system. In *Proc. of the International Conference on Management of Data (SIGMOD)*, pages 541–552, 2013a. DOI: 10.1145/2463676.2465327 98

Michele Dallachiesa, Amr Ebaid, Ahmed Eldawy, Ahmed Elmagarmid, Ihab F. Ilyas, Mourad Ouzzani, and Nan Tang. Nadeef: A commodity data cleaning system. In *Proc. of the International Conference on Management of Data (SIGMOD)*, pages 541–552, 2013b. DOI: 10.1145/2463676.2465327 89

Tamraparni Dasu, Theodore Johnson, S. Muthukrishnan, and Vladislav Shkapenyuk. Mining database structure; or, how to build a data quality browser. In *Proc. of the International Conference on Management of Data (SIGMOD)*, pages 240–251, 2002. DOI: 10.1145/564691.564719 89, 97, 106

Tamraparni Dasu, Theodore Johnson, and Amit Marathe. Database exploration using database dynamics. *IEEE Data Engineering Bulletin*, 29(2):43–59, 2006. 17, 97

Scott Davies and Stuart Russell. P-completeness of searches for smallest possible feature sets. *Technical Report*, Computer Science Division, University of California, 1994. 29

János Demetrovics and Vu Duc Thi. Some remarks on generating Armstrong and inferring functional dependencies relation. *Acta Cybernetica*, 12(1):167–180, 1995. 72

120  BIBLIOGRAPHY

Dong Deng, Raul Castro Fernandez, Ziawasch Abedjan, Sibo Wang, Michael Stonebraker, Ahmed K. Elmagarmid, Ihab F. Ilyas, Samuel Madden, Mourad Ouzzani, and Nan Tang. The data civilizer system. In *Proc. of the Conference on Innovative Data Systems Research (CIDR)*, 2017. 88, 97, 106

J. V. Deshpande. On continuity of a partial order. In *Proc. of the American Mathematical Society*, pages 383–386, 1968. DOI: 10.1090/s0002-9939-1968-0236071-7 24

Keith J. Devlin. *Fundamentals of contemporary set theory*, 1st ed., Springer, Heidelberg, 1979. DOI: 10.1007/978-1-4684-0084-7 24

Thierno Diallo, Noel Novelli, and Jean-Marc Petit. Discovering (frequent) constant conditional functional dependencies. *International Journal of Data Mining, Modelling and Management (IJDMMM)*, 4(3):205–223, 2012. DOI: 10.1504/ijdmmm.2012.048104 77, 89, 90

Jim Diederich and Jack Milton. New methods and fast algorithms for database normalization. *ACM Transactions on Database Systems (TODS)*, 13(3):339–365, 1988. DOI: 10.1145/44498.44499 89

Hong Hai Do and Erhard Rahm. COMA—A system for flexible combination of schema matching approaches. In *Proc. of the International Conference on Very Large Databases (VLDB)*, pages 610–621, 2002. DOI: 10.1016/b978-155860869-6/50060-3 92

Rodney G. Downey and M. R. Fellows. *Parameterized Complexity*, 1st ed., Springer, Heidelberg, 1999. DOI: 10.1007/978-1-4612-0515-9 29

Marianne Durand and Philippe Flajolet. Loglog counting of large cardinalities (extended abstract). In *Proc. of European Symposium on Algorithms (ESA)*, pages 605–617, 2003. DOI: 10.1007/978-3-540-39658-1_55 17

Martin Ester, Hans-Peter Kriegel, Jörg Sander, Michael Wimmer, and Xiaowei Xu. Incremental clustering for mining in a data warehousing environment. In *Proc. of the International Conference on Very Large Databases (VLDB)*, pages 323–333, 1998. 103

Jérôme Euzenat and Pavel Shvaiko. *Ontology Matching*, 2nd ed., Springer, 2013. DOI: 10.1007/978-3-642-38721-0 106

Ronald Fagin. Multivalued dependencies and a new normal form for relational databases. *ACM Transactions on Database Systems (TODS)*, 2(3):262–278, 1977. DOI: 10.1145/320557.320571 85

Wenfei Fan. Dependencies revisited for improving data quality. In *Proc. of the Symposium on Principles of Database Systems (PODS)*, pages 159–170, 2008. DOI: 10.1145/1376916.1376940 79, 89, 90

Wenfei Fan, Floris Geerts, and Xibei Jia. Semandaq: A data quality system based on conditional functional dependencies. *Proc. of the VLDB Endowment*, 1(2):1460–1463, 2008a. DOI: 10.14778/1454159.1454200 98

Wenfei Fan, Floris Geerts, Xibei Jia, and Anastasios Kementsietsidis. Conditional functional dependencies for capturing data inconsistencies. *ACM Transactions on Database Systems (TODS)*, 33(2):1–48, 2008b. DOI: 10.1145/1366102.1366103 10, 76

Wenfei Fan, Floris Geerts, Jianzhong Li, and Ming Xiong. Discovering conditional functional dependencies. *IEEE Transactions on Knowledge and Data Engineering (TKDE)*, 23(5):683–698, 2011. DOI: 10.1109/tkde.2010.154 77, 90

Wenfei Fan, Jianzhong Li, Nan Tang, and Wenyuan Yu. Incremental detection of inconsistencies in distributed data. In *Proc. of the International Conference on Data Engineering (ICDE)*, pages 318–329, 2012. DOI: 10.1109/icde.2012.82 104

Wenfei Fan, Zhe Fan, Chao Tian, and Xin Luna Dong. Keys for graphs. *Proc. of the VLDB Endowment*, 8(12):1590–1601, 2015. DOI: 10.14778/2824032.2824056 95

Wenfei Fan, Yinghui Wu, and Jingbo Xu. Functional dependencies for graphs. In *Proc. of the International Conference on Management of Data (SIGMOD)*, pages 1843–1857, 2016. DOI: 10.1145/2882903.2915232 95

Wenfei Fan, Chunming Hu, Xueli Liu, and Ping Lu. Discovering graph functional dependencies. In *Proc. of the International Conference on Management of Data (SIGMOD)*, pages 427–439, 2018. DOI: 10.1145/3183713.3196916 96

Raul Castro Fernandez, Ziawasch Abedjan, Samuel Madden, and Michael Stonebraker. Towards large-scale data discovery: Position paper. In *Proc. of the International Workshop on Exploratory Search in Databases and the Web (ExploreDB)*, pages 3–5, 2016. DOI: 10.1145/2948674.2948675 97

Raul Castro Fernandez, Ziawasch Abedjan, Famien Koko, Gina Yuan, Samuel Madden, and Michael Stonebraker. Aurum: A data discovery system. In *Proc. of the International Conference on Data Engineering (ICDE)*, 2018. 88, 105

Henning Fernau. Algorithms for learning regular expressions from positive data. *Information and Computation*, 207(4):521–541, 2009. DOI: 10.1016/j.ic.2008.12.008 15

Peter A. Flach and Iztok Savnik. Database dependency discovery: A machine learning approach. *AI Communications*, 12(3):139–160, 1999. 37, 40, 50, 86

Philippe Flajolet and G. Nigel Martin. Probabilistic counting algorithms for data base applications. *Journal of Computer and System Sciences*, 31(2):182–209, 1985. DOI: 10.1016/0022-0000(85)90041-8 17

Philippe Flajolet, Eric Fusy, Olivier Gandouet, and Frédéric Meunier. HyperLogLog: The analysis of a near-optimal cardinality estimation algorithm. In *Proc. of the International Conference on Analysis of Algorithms (AofA)*, pages 127–146, 2007. 17

Luis Galárraga, Christina Teflioudi, Katja Hose, and Fabian M. Suchanek. Fast rule mining in ontological knowledge bases with amie$$+$$+. *VLDB Journal*, 24(6):707–730, December 2015. DOI: 10.1007/s00778-015-0394-1 94

Sumit Ganguly. Counting distinct items over update streams. *Theoretical Computer Science*, 378(3):211–222, 2007. DOI: 10.1016/j.tcs.2007.02.031 103

Hector Garcia-Molina, Jeffrey D. Ullman, and Jennifer Widom. *Database Systems: The Complete Book*, 2nd ed., Prentice Hall Press, Upper Saddle River, NJ, 2008. 30, 85

Eve Garnaud, Nicolas Hanusse, Sofian Maabout, and Noel Novelli. Parallel mining of dependencies. In *Proc. of the International Conference on High Performance Computing and Simulation (HPCS)*, pages 491–498, 2014. DOI: 10.1109/hpcsim.2014.6903725 40

Minos Garofalakis, Daniel Keren, and Vasilis Samoladas. Sketch-based geometric monitoring of distributed stream queries. *Proc. of the VLDB Endowment*, 6(10), 2013. DOI: 10.14778/2536206.2536220 17

Stella Giannakopoulou, Manos Karpathiotakis, Benjamin Gaidioz, and Anastasia Ailamaki. Cleanm: An optimizable query language for unified scale-out data cleaning. *Proc. of the VLDB Endowment*, 10(11):1466–1477, 2017. DOI: 10.14778/3137628.3137654 90

Chris Giannella and Catherine M. Wyss. Finding minimal keys in a relation instance, 1999. http://www.scientificcommons.org/42934961 34

Seymour Ginsburg and Richard Hull. Order dependency in the relational model. *Theoretical Computer Science*, 26(1–2):149–195, 1983. DOI: 10.1016/0304-3975(83)90084-1 82

Lukasz Golab and M. Tamer Özsu. *Data Stream Management*. Morgan Claypool Publishers, 2010. DOI: 10.2200/s00284ed1v01y201006dtm005 104

Lukasz Golab, Howard Karloff, Flip Korn, Divesh Srivastava, and Bei Yu. On generating near-optimal tableaux for conditional functional dependencies. *Proc. of the VLDB Endowment*, 1(1):376–390, 2008. DOI: 10.14778/1453856.1453900 77

Lukasz Golab, Howard Karloff, Flip Korn, Avishek Saha, and Divesh Srivastava. Sequential dependencies. *Proc. of the VLDB Endowment*, 2(1):574–585, 2009. DOI: 10.14778/1687627.1687693 83, 95

Lukasz Golab, Howard Karloff, Flip Korn, and Divesh Srivastava. Data Auditor: Exploring data quality and semantics using pattern tableaux. *Proc. of the VLDB Endowment*, 3(1–2):1641–1644, 2010. DOI: 10.14778/1920841.1921060 89, 98

Lukasz Golab, Flip Korn, and Divesh Srivastava. Efficient and effective analysis of data quality using pattern tableaux. *IEEE Data Engineering Bulletin*, 34(3):26–33, 2011a. 89

Lukasz Golab, Flip Korn, and Divesh Srivastava. Discovering pattern tableaux for data quality analysis: A case study. In *Proc. of the International Workshop on Quality in Databases (QDB)*, pages 47–53, 2011b. 16

Gösta Grahne and Jianfei Zhu. Discovering approximate keys in XML data. In *Proc. of the International Conference on Information and Knowledge Management (CIKM)*, pages 453–460, 2002. DOI: 10.1145/584865.584867 93

Jim Gray, Surajit Chaudhuri, Adam Bosworth, Andrew Layman, Don Reichart, Murali Venka-trao, Frank Pellow, and Hamid Pirahesh. Data Cube: A relational aggregation operator gener-alizing group-by, cross-tab, and sub totals. *Data Mining and Knowledge Discovery*, 1(1):29–53, 1997. DOI: 10.1109/icde.1996.492099 33

Jarek Gryz. Query folding with inclusion dependencies. In *Proc. of the International Conference on Data Engineering (ICDE)*, pages 126–133, 1998. DOI: 10.1109/icde.1998.655768 91

Jarek Gryz. Query rewriting using views in the presence of functional and inclusion dependen-cies. *Information Systems (IS)*, 24(7):597–612, 1999. DOI: 10.1016/s0306-4379(99)00034-4 90

Dimitrios Gunopulos, Roni Khardon, Heikki Mannila, and Ram Sewak Sharma. Discovering all most specific sentences. *ACM Transactions on Database Systems (TODS)*, 28:140–174, 2003. DOI: 10.1145/777943.777945 29

Peter J. Haas, Jeffrey F. Naughton, S. Seshadri, and Lynne Stokes. Sampling-based estimation of the number of distinct values of an attribute. In *Proc. of the International Conference on Very Large Databases (VLDB)*, pages 311–322, 1995. 16

Jean-Luc Hainaut, Jean Henrard, Vincent Englebert, Didier Roland, and Jean-Marc Hick. Database reverse engineering. In *Encyclopedia of Database Systems*, pages 723–728, Springer, Heidelberg, 2009. DOI: 10.1007/978-1-4899-7993-3_646-2 5

Jiawei Han, Micheline Kamber, and Jian Pei. *Data Mining: Concepts and Techniques*. Morgan Kaufmann, 2011. 4

Pat Hanrahan. Analytic database technology for a new kind of user—The data enthusiast. In *Proc. of the International Conference on Management of Data (SIGMOD)*, pages 577–578, 2012. DOI: 10.1145/2213836.2213902 4

Hazar Harmouch and Felix Naumann. Cardinality estimation: An experimental survey. *PVLDB*, 11(4):499–512, 2017. http://www.vldb.org/pvldb/vol11/p499-harmouch.pdf 17

Sven Hartmann and Sebastian Link.  On a problem of fagin concerning multivalued dependencies in relational databases.  *Theory Computer Science*, 353(1):53–62, 2006. DOI: 10.1016/j.tcs.2005.08.036 86

Sven Hartmann, Henning Köhler, Uwe Leck, Sebastian Link, Bernhard Thalheim, and Jing Wang.  Constructing Armstrong tables for general cardinality constraints and not-null constraints.  *Annals of Mathematics and Artificial Intelligence*, 73(1–2):139–165, 2015. DOI: 10.1007/s10472-014-9423-9 110

Jian He, Enzo Veltri, Donatello Santoro, Guoliang Li, Giansalvatore Mecca, Paolo Papotti, and Nan Tang. Interactive and deterministic data cleaning. In *Proc. of the International Conference on Management of Data (SIGMOD)*, pages 893–907, 2016. DOI: 10.1145/2882903.2915242 105

Jan Hegewald, Felix Naumann, and Melanie Weis. XStruct: Efficient schema extraction from multiple and large XML databases. In *Proc. of the International Workshop on Database Interoperability (InterDB)*, 2006. DOI: 10.1109/icdew.2006.166 93

Arvid Heise, Jorge Arnulfo Quiané-Ruiz, Ziawasch Abedjan, Anja Jentzsch, and Felix Naumann.  Scalable discovery of unique column combinations. *Proc. of the VLDB Endowment*, 7(4), 2013. DOI: 10.14778/2732240.2732248 9, 28, 31, 35, 37, 97

Joseph M. Hellerstein, Christopher Ré, Florian Schoppmann, Daisy Zhe Wang, Eugene Fratkin, Aleksander Gorajek, Kee Siong Ng, Caleb Welton, Xixuan Feng, Kun Li, and Arun Kumar. The MADlib analytics library or MAD skills, the SQL. *Proc. of the VLDB Endowment*, 5(12):1700–1711, 2012. DOI: 10.14778/2367502.2367510 99

David I. Holmes.  Authorship attribution. *Computers and the Humanities*, 28:87–106, 1994. DOI: 10.1007/bf01830689 96

Ming Hua and Jian Pei. Cleaning disguised missing data: A heuristic approach. In *Proc. of the International Conference on Knowledge discovery and data mining (SIGKDD)*, pages 950–958, 2007. DOI: 10.1145/1281192.1281294 15

Ykä Huhtala, Juha Kärkkäinen, Pasi Porkka, and Hannu Toivonen. TANE: An efficient algorithm for discovering functional and approximate dependencies. *Computer Journal*, 42(2):100–111, 1999. DOI: 10.1093/comjnl/42.2.100 6, 9, 28, 29, 39, 41, 76, 97

Andrew Ilyas, Joana M. F. da Trindade, Raul C. Fernandez, and Samuel Madden.  Extracting syntactic patterns from databases. In *Proc. of the International Conference on Data Engineering (ICDE)*, 2018. 15

Ihab F. Ilyas and Xu Chu.  Trends in cleaning relational data: Consistency and deduplication. *Foundations and Trends in Databases*, 5(4):281–393, 2015. DOI: 10.1561/1900000045 90

Ihab F. Ilyas, Volker Markl, Peter J. Haas, Paul Brown, and Ashraf Aboulnaga. CORDS: Automatic discovery of correlations and soft functional dependencies. In *Proc. of the International Conference on Management of Data (SIGMOD)*, pages 647–658, Paris, France, 2004. DOI: 10.1145/1007568.1007641 10, 83, 99

Yannis Ioannidis. The history of histograms (abridged). In *Proc. of the International Conference on Very Large Databases (VLDB)*, pages 19–30, Berlin, Germany, 2003. DOI: 10.1016/b978-012722442-8/50011-2 13

Theodore Johnson. Data Profiling, *Encyclopedia of Database Systems*, pages 604–608. Springer, Heidelberg, 2009. DOI: 10.1007/978-1-4899-7993-3_601-2 1, 87

Holger Kache, Wook-Shin Han, Volker Markl, Vijayshankar Raman, and Stephan Ewen. POP/FED: Progressive query optimization for federated queries in DB2. In *Proc. of the International Conference on Very Large Databases (VLDB)*, pages 1175–1178, 2006. DOI: 10.1007/11687238_50 4

Sean Kandel, Andreas Paepcke, Joseph Hellerstein, and Jeffrey Heer. Wrangler: Interactive visual specification of data transformation scripts. In *Proc. of the International Conference on Human Factors in Computing Systems (CHI)*, pages 3363–3372, 2011. DOI: 10.1145/1978942.1979444 97

Sean Kandel, Ravi Parikh, Andreas Paepcke, Joseph Hellerstein, and Jeffrey Heer. Profiler: Integrated statistical analysis and visualization for data quality assessment. In *Proc. of Advanced Visual Interfaces (AVI)*, pages 547–554, 2012. DOI: 10.1145/2254556.2254659 5, 89, 107

Jaewoo Kang and Jeffrey F. Naughton. On schema matching with opaque column names and data values. In *Proc. of the International Conference on Management of Data (SIGMOD)*, pages 205–216, 2003. DOI: 10.1145/872781.872783 13, 92

Jaewoo Kang and Jeffrey F. Naughton. Schema matching using interattribute dependencies. *IEEE Transactions on Knowledge and Data Engineering (TKDE)*, 20(10):1393–1407, 2008. DOI: 10.1109/tkde.2008.100 92

Martti Kantola, Heikki Mannila, R. Kari-Jouko, and Harri Siirtola. Discovering functional and inclusion dependencies in relational databases. *International Journal of Intelligent Systems*, 7(7):591–607, 1992. DOI: 10.1002/int.4550070703 29

Daniel A. Keim and Daniela Oelke. Literature fingerprinting: A new method for visual literary analysis. In *Proc. of Visual Analytics Science and Technology (VAST)*, pages 115–122, Sacramento, CA, 2007. DOI: 10.1109/vast.2007.4389004 96

Nodira Khoussainova, Magdalena Balazinska, and Dan Suciu. Towards correcting input data errors probabilistically using integrity constraints. In *ACM International Workshop on Data Engineering for Wireless and Mobile Access (MobiDE)*, pages 43–50, 2006. DOI: 10.1145/1140104.1140114 98

Jyrki Kivinen and Heikki Mannila.    Approximate inference of functional dependencies from relations. *Theoretical Computer Science*, 149(1):129–149, 1995. DOI: 10.1016/0304-3975(95)00028-u 76, 83

Andreas Koeller and Eelke A. Rundensteiner. Discovery of high-dimensional inclusion dependencies. *Technical Report*, Department of Computer Science, Worcester Polytechnic Institute, 2002. DOI: 10.1109/icde.2003.1260834 71

Andreas Koeller and Elke A. Rundensteiner. Discovery of high-dimensional inclusion dependencies. In *Proc. of the International Conference on Data Engineering (ICDE)*, pages 683–685, 2003. DOI: 10.1109/icde.2003.1260834 56, 70

Henning Köhler and Sebastian Link.  SQL schema design: Foundations, normal forms, and normalization. In *Proc. of the International Conference on Management of Data (SIGMOD)*, pages 267–279, 2016. DOI: 10.1145/2882903.2915239 31

Henning Köhler, Sebastian Link, and Xiaofang Zhou. Possible and certain SQL keys. *Proc. of the VLDB Endowment*, 8(11):1118–1129, 2015. DOI: 10.14778/2809974.2809975 31

Flip Korn, Barna Saha, Divesh Srivastava, and Shanshan Ying. On repairing structural problems in semi-structured data. *Proc. of the VLDB Endowment*, 6(9):601–612, 2013. DOI: 10.14778/2536360.2536361 93

Nick Koudas, Avishek Saha, Divesh Srivastava, and Suresh Venkatasubramanian. Metric functional dependencies. In *Proc. of the International Conference on Data Engineering (ICDE)*, pages 1275–1278, 2009. DOI: 10.1109/icde.2009.219 78

Sebastian Kruse and Felix Naumann. Efficient discovery of approximate dependencies. *Proc. of the VLDB Endowment*, 11(7):759–772, 2018. DOI: 10.14778/3192965.3192968 76

Sebastian Kruse, Thorsten Papenbrock, and Felix Naumann.  Scaling out the discovery of inclusion dependencies. In *Proc. of the Conference Datenbanksysteme in Business, Technologie und Web Technik (BTW)*, pages 445–454, 2015a. 56, 68

Sebastian Kruse, Paolo Papotti, and Felix Naumann.  Estimating data integration and cleaning effort. In *Proc. of the International Conference on Extending Database Technology (EDBT)*, pages 61–72, 2015b. 106

Sebastian Kruse, David Hahn, Marius Walter, and Felix Naumann. Metacrate: Organize and analyze millions of data profiles. In *Proc. of the International Conference on Information and Knowledge Management (CIKM)*, pages 2483–2486, 2017a. DOI: 10.1145/3132847.3133180 106, 107

Sebastian Kruse, Thorsten Papenbrock, Christian Dullweber, Moritz Finke, Manuel Hegner, Martin Zabel, Christian Zoellner, and Felix Naumann. Fast approximate discovery of inclusion dependencies. In *Proc. of the Conference Datenbanksysteme in Business, Technologie und Web Technik (BTW)*, pages 207–226, 2017b. 83

Douglas Laney. 3D data management: Controlling data volume, velocity and variety. *Technical Report*, Gartner, 2001. 5

Philipp Langer and Felix Naumann. Efficient order dependency detection. *VLDB Journal*, 25(2):223–241, 2016. DOI: 10.1007/s00778-015-0412-3 82

Van Bao Tran Le, Sebastian Link, and Flavio Ferrarotti. Empirical evidence for the usefulness of armstrong tables in the acquisition of semantically meaningful SQL constraints. *Data and Knowledge Engineering (DKE)*, 98:74–103, 2015. DOI: 10.1016/j.datak.2015.07.006 31

Mark Levene and Millist W. Vincent. Justification for inclusion dependency normal form. *IEEE Transactions on Knowledge and Data Engineering (TKDE)*, 12:2000, 1999. DOI: 10.1109/69.842267 89

Weibang Li, Zhanhuai Li, Qun Chen, Tao Jiang, and Hailong Liu. Discovering functional dependencies in vertically distributed big data. *Proc. of the International Conference on Web Information Systems Engineering (WISE)*, pages 199–207, 2015. DOI: 10.1007/978-3-319-26187-4_15 40

Yunyao Li, Rajasekar Krishnamurthy, Sriram Raghavan, Shivakumar Vaithyanathan, and H. V. Jagadish. Regular expression learning for information extraction. In *Proc. of the Conference on Empirical Methods in Natural Language Processing (EMNLP)*, pages 21–30, 2008. DOI: 10.3115/1613715.1613719 15

Bing Liu. Sentiment analysis and subjectivity. *Handbook of Natural Language Processing*, 2nd ed., Chapman and Hall/CRC, New York, 2010. 96

Jixue Liu, Jiuyong Li, Chengfei Liu, and Yongfeng Chen. Discover dependencies from data— A review. *IEEE Transactions on Knowledge and Data Engineering (TKDE)*, 24(2):251–264, 2012. DOI: 10.1109/tkde.2010.197 26, 29

Stéphane Lopes, Jean-Marc Petit, and Lotfi Lakhal. Efficient discovery of functional dependencies and Armstrong relations. In *Proc. of the International Conference on Extending Database Technology (EDBT)*, pages 350–364, 2000. DOI: 10.1007/3-540-46439-5_24 39, 40, 46

Stéphane Lopes, Jean-Marc Petit, and Farouk Toumani. Discovering interesting inclusion dependencies: Application to logical database tuning. *Information Systems (IS)*, 27(1):1–19, 2002. DOI: 10.1016/s0306-4379(01)00027-8 9, 72

Claudio L. Lucchesi and Sylvia L. Osborn. Candidate keys for relations. *Journal of Computer and System Sciences*, 17(2):270–279, 1978. DOI: 10.1016/0022-0000(78)90009-0 22

Jayant Madhavan, Philip A. Bernstein, and Erhard Rahm. Generic schema matching with cupid. In *Proc. of the International Conference on Very Large Databases (VLDB)*, pages 49–58, 2001. 92

Michael V. Mannino, Paicheng Chu, and Thomas Sager. Statistical profile estimation in database systems. *ACM Computing Surveys*, 20(3):191–221, 1988. DOI: 10.1145/62061.62063 4

Fabien De Marchi and Jean-Marc Petit. Zigzag: A new algorithm for mining large inclusion dependencies in databases. In *Proc. of the International Conference on Data Mining (ICDM)*, pages 27–34, 2003. DOI: 10.1109/icdm.2003.1250899 28, 56, 71

Fabien De Marchi, Stéphane Lopes, and Jean-Marc Petit. Efficient algorithms for mining inclusion dependencies. In *Proc. of the International Conference on Extending Database Technology (EDBT)*, pages 464–476, 2002. DOI: 10.1007/3-540-45876-x_30 9

Fabien De Marchi, Stéphane Lopes, and Jean-Marc Petit. Unary and n-ary inclusion dependency discovery in relational databases. *Journal of Intelligent Information Systems*, 32:53–73, 2009. DOI: 10.1007/s10844-007-0048-x 23, 56, 61, 69, 76

Fabien De Marchi. CLIM: Closed Inclusion Dependency Mining in Databases. In *ICDM Workshops*, pages 1098–1103, 2011.

Victor M. Markowitz and Johann A. Makowsky. Identifying extended entity-relationship object structures in relational schemas. *IEEE Transactions on Software Engineering*, 16(8):777–790, 1990. DOI: 10.1109/32.57618 5

Arkady Maydanchik. *Data Quality Assessement*. Technics Publications, Westfield, New Jersey, 2007. 4, 11

Ahmed Metwally, Divyakant Agrawal, and Amr El Abbadi. Efficient computation of frequent and top-K elements in data streams. In *ICDT*, pages 398–412, 2005. DOI: 10.1007/978-3-540-30570-5_27 17

Laurent Mignet, Denilson Barbosa, and Pierangelo Veltri. The XML web: A first study. In *Proc. of the International World Wide Web Conference (WWW)*, pages 500–510, 2003. DOI: 10.1145/775220.775223 93

Jayadev Misra and David Gries. Finding repeated elements. *Science of Computer Programming*, 2(2):143–152, 1982. DOI: 10.1016/0167-6423(82)90012-0 17

Irena Mlynkova, Kamil Toman, and Jaroslav Pokorný. Statistical analysis of real XML data collections. In *Proc. of the International Conference on Management of Data (COMAD)*, pages 15–26, 2006. 93

Felix Naumann. Data profiling revisited. *SIGMOD Record*, 42(4), 2013. DOI: 10.1145/2590989.2590995 xv

Wilfred Ng. An extension of the relational data model to incorporate ordered domains. *ACM Transactions on Database Systems*, 26(3):344–383, 2001. DOI: 10.1145/502030.502033 82

Noël Novelli and Rosine Cicchetti. FUN: An efficient algorithm for mining functional and embedded dependencies. In *Proc. of the International Conference on Database Theory (ICDT)*, pages 189–203, 2001. DOI: 10.1007/3-540-44503-x_13 39, 42

Nikos Ntarmos, Peter Triantafillou, and Gerhard Weikum. Distributed hash sketches: Scalable, efficient, and accurate cardinality estimation for distributed multisets. *ACM Transactions on Computer Systems (TOCS)*, 27(1):1–53, 2009. DOI: 10.1145/1482619.1482621 17

Bo Pang and Lillian Lee. Opinion mining and sentiment analysis. *Foundation and Trends in Information Retrieval*, 2(1–2):1–135, 2008. DOI: 10.1561/1500000011 96

Thorsten Papenbrock and Felix Naumann. A hybrid approach to functional dependency discovery. In *Proc. of the International Conference on Management of Data (SIGMOD)*, pages 821–833, 2016. DOI: 10.1145/2882903.2915203 40, 50, 51, 54, 55, 106

Thorsten Papenbrock and Felix Naumann. A hybrid approach for efficient unique column combination discovery. In *Proc. of the Conference Datenbanksysteme in Business, Technologie und Web Technik (BTW)*, pages 195–204, 2017a. 32, 37, 38

Thorsten Papenbrock and Felix Naumann. Data-driven schema normalization. In *Proc. of the International Conference on Extending Database Technology (EDBT)*, pages 342–353, 2017b. 89, 108

Thorsten Papenbrock, Tanja Bergmann, Moritz Finke, Jakob Zwiener, and Felix Naumann. Data profiling with Metanome (demo). *Proc. of the VLDB Endowment*, 8(12):1860–1871, 2015a. DOI: 10.14778/2824032.2824086 97

Thorsten Papenbrock, Jens Ehrlich, Jannik Marten, Tommy Neubert, Jan-Peer Rudolph, Martin Schönberg, Jakob Zwiener, and Felix Naumann. Functional dependency discovery: An experimental evaluation of seven algorithms. *Proc. of the VLDB Endowment*, 8(10):1082–1093, 2015b. DOI: 10.14778/2794367.2794377 9, 30, 31, 41, 54

Thorsten Papenbrock, Arvid Heise, and Felix Naumann. Progressive duplicate detection. *IEEE Transactions on Knowledge and Data Engineering (TKDE)*, 27(5):1316–1329, 2015c. DOI: 10.1109/tkde.2014.2359666 104

Thorsten Papenbrock, Sebastian Kruse, Jorge-Arnulfo Quiané-Ruiz, and Felix Naumann. Divide and conquer-based inclusion dependency discovery. *Proc. of the VLDB Endowment*, 8(7):774–785, 2015d. DOI: 10.14778/2752939.2752946 56, 62, 97

Glenn N. Paulley and Per-Ake Larson. Exploiting uniqueness in query optimization. In *Proc. of the Conference of the Centre for Advanced Studies on Collaborative Research: Distributed Computing*, pages 804–822, 1993. DOI: 10.1145/1925805.1925812 91

Glenn Norman Paulley. Exploiting functional dependence in query optimization. *Technical Report*, University of Waterloo, 2000. 91

Jean-Marc Petit, Jacques Kouloumdjian, Jean-François Boulicaut, and Farouk Toumani. Using queries to improve database reverse engineering. In *Proc. of the International Conference on Conceptual Modeling (ER)*, pages 369–386, 1994. DOI: 10.1007/3-540-58786-1_91 5

Gregory Piatetsky-Shapiro and Christopher Matheus. Measuring data dependencies in large databases. In *Proc. of the AAAI Knowledge Discovery in Databases Workshop*, pages 162–173, 1993. 108

Leo Pipino, Yang Lee, and Richard Wang. Data quality assessment. *Communications of the ACM*, 4:211–218, 2002. DOI: 10.1145/505999.506010 5

Viswanath Poosala, Peter J. Haas, Yannis E. Ioannidis, and Eugene J. Shekita. Improved histograms for selectivity estimation of range predicates. In *Proc. of the International Conference on Management of Data (SIGMOD)*, pages 294–305, Montreal, Canada, 1996. DOI: 10.1145/235968.233342 4

Gil Press. Cleaning data: Most time-consuming, least enjoyable data science task. *Forbes*, March 2016. 1

Abdulhakim Ali Qahtan, Ahmed K. Elmagarmid, Raul Castro Fernandez, Mourad Ouzzani, and Nan Tang. Fahes: A robust disguised missing values detector. In *Proc. of the International Conference on Knowledge discovery and data mining (SIGKDD)*, pages 2100–2109, 2018. DOI: 10.1145/3219819.3220109 16

Erhard Rahm and Philip A. Bernstein. A survey of approaches to automatic schema matching. *Proc. of the VLDB Endowment*, 10(4):334–350, 2001. DOI: 10.1007/s007780100057 91

Erhard Rahm and Hong-Hai Do. Data cleaning: Problems and current approaches. *IEEE Data Engineering Bulletin*, 23(4):3–13, 2000. 3

Vijayshankar Raman and Joseph M. Hellerstein. Potter's Wheel: An interactive data cleaning system. In *Proc. of the International Conference on Very Large Databases (VLDB)*, pages 381–390, Rome, Italy, 2001. 7, 14, 89, 97

Theodoros Rekatsinas, Xu Chu, Ihab F. Ilyas, and Christopher Ré. Holoclean: Holistic data repairs with probabilistic inference. *Proc. of the VLDB Endowment*, 10(11):1190–1201, 2017. DOI: 10.14778/3137628.3137631 90

Alexandra Rostin, Oliver Albrecht, Jana Bauckmann, Felix Naumann, and Ulf Leser. A machine learning approach to foreign key discovery. In *Proc. of the ACM SIGMOD Workshop on the Web and Databases (WebDB)*, 2009. 9, 88, 107

Arnaud Sahuguet and Fabien Azavant. Building light-weight wrappers for legacy web data-sources using W4F. In *Proc. of the International Conference on Very Large Databases (VLDB)*, pages 738–741, 1999. 93

Hossein Saiedian and Thomas Spencer. An efficient algorithm to compute the candidate keys of a relational database schema. *The Computer Journal*, 39(2):124–132, 1996. DOI: 10.1093/comjnl/39.2.124 88

Sunita Sarawagi. Information extraction. *Foundations and Trends in Databases*, 1(3):261–377, 2008. DOI: 10.1561/1900000003 96

Iztok Savnik and Peter A. Flach. Discovery of multivalued dependencies from relations. *Journal of Intelligent Data Analysis*, 4:195–211, 2000. DOI: 10.3233/ida-2000-43-403 86

Nuhad Shaabani and Christoph Meinel. Scalable inclusion dependency discovery. In *Proc. of the International Conference on Database Systems for Advanced Applications (DASFAA)*, pages 425–440, 2015. DOI: 10.1007/978-3-319-18120-2_25 56, 66

Nuhad Shaabani and Christoph Meinel. Detecting maximum inclusion dependencies without candidate generation. In *Proc. of the International Conference on Database and Expert Systems Applications (DEXA)*, pages 118–133, 2016. DOI: 10.1007/978-3-319-44406-2_10 56, 72

Yannis Sismanis, Paul Brown, Peter J. Haas, and Berthold Reinwald. GORDIAN: Efficient and scalable discovery of composite keys. In *Proc. of the VLDB Endowment*, pages 691–702, 2006. 6, 31, 32, 33

Kenneth P. Smith, Michael Morse, Peter Mork, Maya Hao Li, Arnon Rosenthal, M. David Allen, and Len Seligman. The role of schema matching in large enterprises. In *Proc. of the Conference on Innovative Data Systems Research (CIDR)*, Asilomar, CA, 2009. 106

Shaoxu Song and Lei Chen. Discovering matching dependencies. In *Proc. of the International Conference on Information and Knowledge Management (CIKM)*, pages 1421–1424, 2009. DOI: 10.1145/1645953.1646135 80

Michael Stonebraker, Daniel Bruckner, Ihab F. Ilyas, George Beskales, Mitch Cherniack, Stan Zdonik, Alexander Pagan, and Shan Xu. Data curation at scale: The Data Tamer system. In *Proc. of the Conference on Innovative Data Systems Research (CIDR)*, Asilomar, CA, 2013. 10

Jaroslaw Szlichta, Parke Godfrey, and Jarek Gryz. Fundamentals of order dependencies. *Proc. of the VLDB Endowment*, 5(11):1220–1231, 2012. DOI: 10.14778/2350229.2350241 82

Jaroslaw Szlichta, Parke Godfrey, Jarek Gryz, and Calisto Zuzarte. Expressiveness and complexity of order dependencies. *Proc. of the VLDB Endowment*, 6(14):1858–1869, 2013. DOI: 10.14778/2556549.2556568 82

Jaroslaw Szlichta, Parke Godfrey, Lukasz Golab, Mehdi Kargar, and Divesh Srivastava. Effective and complete discovery of order dependencies via set-based axiomatization. *Proc. of the VLDB Endowment*, 10(7):721–732, 2017. DOI: 10.14778/3067421.3067422 81, 82, 84

Jaroslaw Szlichta, Parke Godfrey, Lukasz Golab, Mehdi Kargar, and Divesh Srivastava. Effective and complete discovery of bidirectional order dependencies via set-based axioms. *VLDB Journal*, to appear, 2018. DOI: 10.1007/s00778-018-0510-0 82

Saravanan Thirumuruganathan, Laure Berti-Equille, Mourad Ouzzani, Jorge-Arnulfo Quiane-Ruiz, and Nan Tang. UGuide: User-guided discovery of FD-detectable errors. In *Proc. of the International Conference on Management of Data (SIGMOD)*, pages 1385–1397, 2017. DOI: 10.1145/3035918.3064024 105

David Toman and Grant Weddell. On keys and functional dependencies as first-class citizens in description logics. *Journal of Automated Reasoning*, 40(2):117–132, 2008. DOI: 10.1007/s10817-007-9092-z 19

Pauray S. M. Tsai, Chih-Chong Lee, and Arbee L. P. Chen. An efficient approach for incremental association rule mining. In *Methodologies for Knowledge Discovery and Data Mining*, vol. 1574 of *Lecture Notes in Computer Science*, pages 74–83, Springer Berlin Heidelberg, 1999. DOI: 10.1007/3-540-48912-6_10 103

Jeffrey D. Ullman. *Principles of Database and Knowledge-Base Systems: Volume II: The New Technologies.* W. H. Freeman and Company, New York, 1990. 21, 85

Jeffrey D. Ullman. *Information Integration using Logical Views*, pages 19–40. Springer, Heidelberg, 1997. DOI: 10.1007/3-540-62222-5_34 91

Millist W. Vincent, Jixue Liu, and Chengfei Liu. Strong functional dependencies and their application to normal forms in XML. *ACM Transactions on Database Systems (TODS)*, 29(3):445–462, 2004. DOI: 10.1145/1016028.1016029 93

Larysa Visengeriyeva and Ziawasch Abedjan. Metadata-driven error detection. In *Proc. of the International Conference on Scientific and Statistical Database Management (SSDBM)*, 2018. DOI: 10.1145/3221269.3223028 90

Tobias Vogel and Felix Naumann. Instance-based "one-to-some" assignment of similarity measures to attributes. In *Proc. of the International Conference on Cooperative Information Systems (CoopIS)*, pages 412–420, 2011. DOI: 10.1007/978-3-642-25109-2_27 15

Shyue-Liang Wang, Wen-Chieh Tsou, Jiann-Horng Lin, and Tzung-Pei Hong. Maintenance of discovered functional dependencies: Incremental deletion. In *Intelligent Systems Design and Applications*, vol. 23 of *Advances in Soft Computing*, pages 579–588, Springer Berlin Heidelberg, 2003. DOI: 10.1007/978-3-540-44999-7_55 103

Kyu-Young Whang, Brad T. Vander Zanden, and Howard M. Taylor. A linear-time probabilistic counting algorithm for database applications. *ACM Transactions on Database Systems (TODS)*, 15(2):208–229, 1990. DOI: 10.1145/78922.78925 17

Steven Euijong Whang, David Marmaros, and Hector Garcia-Molina. Pay-as-you-go entity resolution. *IEEE Transactions on Knowledge and Data Engineering (TKDE)*, 25(5):1111–1124, 2013. DOI: 10.1109/tkde.2012.43 104

Jef Wijsen. *Temporal Dependencies*, pages 2960–2966. Springer, Boston, MA, 2009. DOI: 10.1007/978-0-387-39940-9_39 80, 81

Catharine Wyss, Chris Giannella, and Edward Robertson. FastFDs: A heuristic-driven, depth-first algorithm for mining functional dependencies from relation instances extended abstract. In *Proc. of the International Conference of Data Warehousing and Knowledge Discovery (DaWaK)*, pages 101–110, 2001. DOI: 10.1007/3-540-44801-2_11 39, 40, 48

Mohamed Yakout, Ahmed K. Elmagarmid, Jennifer Neville, and Mourad Ouzzani. GDR: A system for guided data repair. In *Proc. of the International Conference on Management of Data (SIGMOD)*, pages 1223–1226, 2010. DOI: 10.1145/1807167.1807325 98

Men Hin Yan and Ada Wai-chee Fu. Algorithm for discovering multivalued dependencies. In *Proc. of the International Conference on Information and Knowledge Management (CIKM)*, pages 556–558, 2001. DOI: 10.1145/502684.502688 86

Hong Yao and Howard J. Hamilton. Mining functional dependencies from data. *Data Mining and Knowledge Discovery*, 16(2):197–219, 2008. DOI: 10.1007/s10618-007-0083-9 9

Hong Yao, Howard J. Hamilton, and Cory J. Butz. FD_Mine: Discovering functional dependencies in a database using equivalences. In *Proc. of the International Conference on Data Mining (ICDM)*, pages 729–732, 2002. DOI: 10.1109/icdm.2002.1184040 39, 45

Cong Yu and H. V. Jagadish. Efficient discovery of XML data redundancies. In *Proc. of the International Conference on Very Large Databases (VLDB)*, pages 103–114, 2006. 93

Ehtisham Zaidi, Rita L. Sallam, and Shubhangi Vashisth. Market guide for data preparation, 2017. https://www.gartner.com/doc/3838463/market-guide-data-preparation 99

Carlo Zaniolo. Database relations with null values. *Journal of Computer and System Sciences*, 28(1):142–166, 1984. DOI: 10.1016/0022-0000(84)90080-1 30

Meihui Zhang and Kaushik Chakrabarti. InfoGather+: Semantic matching and annotation of numeric and time-varying attributes in web tables. In *Proc. of the International Conference on Management of Data (SIGMOD)*, pages 145–156, 2013. DOI: 10.1145/2463676.2465276 15

Meihui Zhang, Marios Hadjieleftheriou, Beng Chin Ooi, Cecilia M. Procopiuc, and Divesh Srivastava. On multi-column foreign key discovery. *Proc. of the VLDB Endowment*, 3(1–2):805–814, 2010. DOI: 10.14778/1920841.1920944 83, 88, 89, 92, 108

Meihui Zhang, Marios Hadjieleftheriou, Beng Chin Ooi, Cecilia M. Procopiuc, and Divesh Srivastava. Automatic discovery of attributes in relational databases. In *Proc. of the International Conference on Management of Data (SIGMOD)*, pages 109–120, 2011. DOI: 10.1145/1989323.1989336 15

# Authors' Biographies

## ZIAWASCH ABEDJAN

**Ziawasch Abedjan** is Juniorprofessor (Assistant Professor) and Head of the "Big Data Management" (BigDaMa) Group at the Technische Universität Berlin. Before Ziawasch was a postdoc at the "Computer Science and Artificial Intelligence Laboratory" at MIT working on various data integration topics. Ziawasch received his Ph.D. from the Hasso Plattner Institute in Potsdam, Germany. His research interests include, data mining, data integration, and data profiling.

## LUKASZ GOLAB

**Lukasz Golab** is an Associate Professor at the University of Waterloo and a Canada Research Chair. Prior to joining Waterloo, he was a Senior Member of Research Staff at AT&T Labs in Florham Park, NJ, USA. He holds a B.Sc. in Computer Science (with High Distinction) from the University of Toronto and a Ph.D. in Computer Science (with Alumni Gold Medal) from the University of Waterloo. His publications span several research areas within data management and data analytics, including data stream management, data profiling, data quality, data science for social good, and educational data mining.

## FELIX NAUMANN

**Felix Naumann** studied mathematics, economy, and computer sciences at the University of Technology in Berlin. After receiving his diploma in 1997 he joined the graduate school "Distributed Information Systems" at Humboldt University of Berlin. He completed his Ph.D. thesis on "Quality-driven Query Answering" in 2000. In 2001 and 2002 he worked at the IBM Almaden Research Center on topics around data integration. From 2003–2006 he was an assistant professor of information integration at the Humboldt University of Berlin. Since 2006 he has held the chair for information systems at the Hasso Plattner Institute at the University of Potsdam in Germany. He is Editor-in-Chief of the *Information Systems* journal. His research interests are in the areas of information integration, data quality, data cleansing, text extraction, and—of course—data profiling. He has given numerous invited talks and tutorials on the topic of the book.

# THORSTEN PAPENBROCK

**Thorsten Papenbrock** is a researcher and lecturer at the Hasso Plattner Institute at the University of Potsdam in Germany. He received his M.Sc. in IT-Systems Engineering in 2014 and his Ph.D. in Computer Science in 2017. His thesis on "Data Profiling–Efficient Discovery of Dependencies" inspired many sections of this book. In research, his main interests are data profiling, data cleaning, distributed and parallel computing, database systems, and data analytics.

Printed in the United States
by Baker & Taylor Publisher Services